# Salads, Sandwiches and Chafing-Dish Dainties

*With Fifty Illustrations of Original Dishes*

By

Janet McKenzie Hill

# INTRODUCTION.

> At their savory dinner set
> Herbs and other country messes,
> Which the neat-handed Phyllis dresses.
> —*Milton.*

Our taste for salads—and in their simplest form who is not fond of salads?—is an inheritance from classic times and Eastern lands. In the hot climates of the Orient, cucumbers and melons were classed among earth's choicest productions; and a resort ever grateful in the heat of the day was "a lodge in a garden of cucumbers."

At the Passover the Hebrews ate lettuce, camomile, dandelion and mint, —the "bitter herbs" of the Paschal feast,—combined with oil and vinegar. Of the Greeks, the rich were fond of the lettuces of Smyrna, which appeared on their tables at the close of the repast. In this respect the Romans, at first, imitated the Greeks, but later came to serve lettuce with eggs as a first course and to excite the appetite. The ancient physicians valued lettuce for its narcotic virtue, and, on account of this property, Galen, the celebrated Greek physician, called it "the philosopher's or wise man's herb."

The older historians make frequent mention of salad plants and salads. In the biblical narrative Moses wrote: "And the children of Israel wept again and said, We remember the fish which we did eat in Egypt freely; the cucumbers, and the melons, and the leeks, and the onions, and the garlick."

In his second Eclogue, Virgil represents a rustic maid, Thestylis, preparing for the reapers a salad called *moretum*. He wrote, also, a poem bearing this title, in which he describes the composition and preparation of the dish.

A modern authority says, "Salads refresh without exciting and make people younger." Whether this be strictly true or not may be an open question, but certainly in the assertion a grain of truth is visible; for it is a well-known fact that "salad plants are better tonics and blood purifiers than druggists' compounds." There is, also, an old proverb: "Eat onions in May, and all the year after physicians may play." What is health but youth?

Vegetables, fish and meats, "left over,"—all may be transformed, by artistic treatment, into salads delectable to the eye and taste. Potatoes are subject to endless combinations. First of all in this connection, before dressing the potatoes allow them to stand in bouillon, meat broth, or even in the liquor in which corned beef has been cooked; then drain carefully before adding the oil and other seasonings.

Of uncooked vegetables, cabbage lettuce—called long ago by the Greek physician, Galen, the philosopher's or wise man's herb—stands at the head of salad plants. Like all uncooked vegetables, lettuce must be served fresh and crisp, and the more quickly it is grown the more tender it will be. When dressed for the table, each leaf should glisten with oil, yet no perceptible quantity should fall to the salad-bowl. Watercress, being rich in sulphuretted oil, is often served without oil. Cheese or eggs combine well with cress; and such a salad, with a sandwich of coarse bread and butter, together with a cup of sparkling coffee, forms an ideal luncheon for a picnic or for the home piazza. Indeed, all the compound salads,—that is, salads of many ingredients,—more particularly if they are served with a cooked or mayonnaise dressing, are substantial enough for the chief dish of a hearty meal. Their digestibility depends, in large measure, on the tenderness of the different ingredients, as well as upon the freshness of the uncooked vegetables that enter into their composition.

A salad has this superiority over every other production of the culinary art: A salad (but not every salad) is suitable to serve upon any occasion, or to any class or condition of men. Among *bon vivants*, without a *new* salad, no matter how *recherché* the other courses may be, the luncheon, or dinner party, of to-day does not pass as an unqualified success.

While salads may be compounded of all kinds of delicate meats, fish, shellfish, eggs, nuts, fruit, cheese and vegetables, cooked or uncooked, two things are indispensable to every kind and grade of salad, viz., the foundation of vegetables and the dressing.

## The Dressing.

Salads are dressed with oil, acid and condiments; and, sometimes, a sweet, as honey or sugar, is used. A perfect salad is not necessarily acetic. The presence of vinegar in a dressing, like that of onions and its relatives, on most occasions should be suspected only. Wyvern and other true epicures consider the advice of Sydney Smith, as expressed in the following couplet, "most pernicious":—

> "Four times the spoon with oil of Lucca crown,
> And twice with vinegar procured from town."

Aromatic vinegars, a few drops of which, used occasionally, lend piquancy and variety to an every-day salad, can be purchased at high-class provision stores; but the true salad-maker is an artist, and prefers to compound her own colors (*i.e.*, vinegars); therefore we have given several recipes for the same, which may be easily modified to suit individual tastes.

Indeed, the dressing of a salad, though in the early days of the century considered a special art,—an art that rendered it possible for at least one noted Royalist refugee to amass a considerable fortune,—is entirely a matter of individual taste, or, more properly speaking, of cultivation. On this account, particularly for a French dressing, no set rules can be given. By experience and judgment one must decide upon the proportions of the different ingredients, or, more specifically, upon the proportions of the oil and acid to be used. Often four spoonfuls of oil are used to one of vinegar. Four spoonfuls of oil to two, three or four of vinegar may be the proportion preferred by others, and the quantity may vary for different salads.

Though in many of the recipes explicit quantities of oil, vinegar and condiments are given, it is with the understanding that these quantities are indicated simply as an approximate rule; sometimes less and sometimes more will be required, according to the tendency of the article dressed to absorb oil and acid, or the taste of the salad dresser.

## Use of Dressings.

The dressings in most common use are the French and the mayonnaise. A French dressing is used for green vegetables, for fruit and nuts, and to marinate cooked vegetables, or the meat or fish for a meat or fish salad. Mayonnaise dressing is used for meat, fish, some varieties of fruit, as banana, apple and pineapple, and for some vegetables, as cauliflower, asparagus and tomatoes. Any article to be served with mayonnaise, after standing an hour or more in a marinade,—*i.e.*, French dressing,—should be carefully drained, as, by the pickling process, liquid will drain out into the bottom of the vessel and, mixing with the mayonnaise, will liquefy the same.

## Arrangement of Salads.

In the arrangement of salads there may be great display of taste and individuality. By a judicious selection from materials that may be kept constantly in store, and with one or two window boxes, in which herbs are growing, any one, with a modicum of inventive skill, can so change and modify the appearance and flavor of her salads that she may seem always to present a new one.

## Composition of Mayonnaise.

Mayonnaise dressing is composed largely of olive oil. A small amount of yolk of egg is used as a foundation. The oil, with the addition of condiments, is slightly acidulated with vinegar and lemon juice, one or both, and the whole is made very light and thick by beating. Mayonnaise forms a very handsome dressing, and it is much enjoyed by those who are fond of oil.

## Value of Oil.

Pure olive oil is almost entirely without flavor, and a taste for it can be readily acquired; and, when we consider that it contains all the really desirable qualities of the once-famous cod-liver oil, except the phosphates, and that these may be supplied in the other materials of the salad, it would seem wise to cultivate a taste for so wholesome an article. By the addition of cream, in the proportion of a cup of whipped cream to a pint of dressing, those to whom oil has not become agreeable can so modify its "tone" that they too will enjoy the mayonnaise dressing.

## Boiled and Cream Dressings.

For the French and mayonnaise dressings—particularly for the latter—we sometimes substitute a *boiled* and sometimes a *cream* dressing. In the first, butter, or cream, is substituted for oil, and the materials are combined by cooking. In the latter, as the name implies, cream is the basis, and this may be either sweet or sour.

## Important Points in Salad=Making.

(1) The green vegetables should be served fresh and crisp.

(2) Meat and fish should be well marinated and cold.

(3) The ingredients composing the salad should not be combined until the last moment before serving.

## When to Serve Salads with French or Mayonnaise Dressing.

As a rule, subject, however, to exceptions, light vegetable salads, dressed with French dressing, are served at dinner; while heavy meat or fish Salads are reserved for luncheon, or supper, and are served with mayonnaise or cream dressing.

## When to Serve a Fruit Salad.

A fruit salad, with sweet dressing, is served with cake at a luncheon, or supper, or in the evening; that is, it may take the place of fruit in the dessert course. A fruit salad, with French or mayonnaise dressing, may be served as a first course at luncheon, or with the game or roast, though in the latter case the French dressing is preferable.

## Salads with Cheese.

The rightful place of salads is with the roast or game. Here the crisp, green salad herbs, delicately acidulated, complement and correct the richness of these *plats*.

Occasionally when the game is omitted and an acid sauce accompanies the roast, a simple salad combined with cheese in some form, preferably cooked and hot, is selected to lengthen the menu. This same combination of hot cheese dish and salad should be a favorite one for home luncheons, when this meal is not made the children's dinner. The salad too in this combination, aided by the bread accompanying it, corrects by dilution the over concentration and richness of the cheese dish. In England neatly trimmed-and-cleansed celery stalks and cheese often precede the sweet course; but by virtue of its mission as a digester of everything but itself and of the common disinclination to have the taste of sweets linger upon the palate, the place of cheese as cheese is with the coffee.

# HOW TO MAKE AROMATIC VINEGARS, TO KEEP VEGETABLES AND TO PREPARE GARNISHES.

### How to Boil Eggs Hard for Garnishing.

Cover the eggs with boiling water. Set them on the back of the range, where the water will keep hot without boiling, about forty minutes. Cool in cold water, and with a thin, sharp knife cut as desired.

### To Poach Whites of Eggs.

Turn the whites of the eggs into a well-buttered mould or cup, set upon a trivet in a dish of hot water, and cook until firm, either upon the back of the range or in the oven, and without letting the water boil. Turn from the mould, cut into slices, and then into fanciful shapes; or chop fine.

### Royal Custard for Moulds of Aspic.

Beat together one whole egg and three yolks; add one-fourth a teaspoonful, each, of mace, salt and paprica, and, when well mixed, add half a cup of cream. Bake in a buttered mould, set in a pan of water, until firm. When cold cut in thin slices, then stamp out in fanciful shapes with French cutters. Use in decorating a mould for aspic jelly.

## How to Use Garlic or Onion in Salads.

The salad-bowl may be rubbed with the cut surface of a clove of garlic, or a *chapon* may be used. A *chapon*, according to gastronomic usage, is a thin piece of bread rubbed on all sides with the cut surface of a clove of garlic and put into the salad-bowl before the seasonings. It is tossed with the salad and dressings, to which it imparts its flavor. It may be divided and served with the salad. Oftentimes, instead of one piece, several small cubes of bread are thus used.

After a slice of onion has been removed, the cut surface of the onion may be pressed with a rotary motion against a grater and the juice extracted; or a lemon-squeezer kept for this special purpose may be used.

## How to Shell and Blanch Chestnuts.

Score the shell of each nut, and put into a frying-pan with a teaspoonful of butter for each pint of nuts. Shake the pan over the fire until the butter is melted; then set in the oven five minutes. With a sharp knife remove the shells and skins together.

## How to Blanch Walnuts and Almonds.

Put the nut meats over the fire in cold water, bring quickly to the boiling-point, drain, and rinse with cold water, then the skins may be easily rubbed from the almonds; a small pointed knife will be needed for the walnuts.

## How to Chop Fresh Herbs.

Pluck the leaves close, discarding the stems; gather the leaves together closely with the fingers of the left hand, then with a sharp knife cut through close to the fingers; push the leaves out a little and cut again, and so continue until all are cut. Now gather into a mound and chop to a very fine powder, holding the point of the knife close to the board. Put the chopped herb into a cheese-cloth and hold under a stream of cold water, then wring dry. Use this green powder for dusting over a salad when required.

## How to Cut Radishes for a Garnish.

Cut a thin slice from the leaf end of each; cut off the root end so as to leave it the length of the pistil of a flower. With a small, sharp knife score the pink skin, at the root end, into five or six sections extending half-way down the radish; then loosen the skin above these sections. Put the radishes in cold water for a little time, when they will become crisp, and the points will stand out like the petals of a flower.

## How to Clean Lettuce, Endive, Etc.

A short time before serving cut off the roots and freshen the vegetable in cold water. Then break the leaves from the stalk; dip repeatedly into cold water, examining carefully, until perfectly clean, taking care not to crush the leaves. Put into a French wire basket made for the purpose, or into a piece of mosquito netting or cheese-cloth, and shake gently until the water is removed. Then spread on a plate or in a colander and set in a cool place until the moment for serving.

## How to Clean Cress.

Pick over the stalks so as to remove grass, etc. Wash and dry in the same manner as the lettuce, but without removing the leaves from the stems, except when the stems are very coarse and large.

## How to Clean Cabbage and Cauliflower.

Let stand head downwards half an hour in cold salted water, using a tablespoonful of salt to a quart of water.

## How to Render Uncooked Vegetables Crisp.

Put into cold water with a bit of ice and a slice of lemon. When ready to use, dry between folds of cheese-cloth and let stand exposed to the air a few moments.

## How to Blanch and Cook Vegetables for Salads.

Cut the vegetables as desired, in cubes, lozenges, balls, *juliennes*, etc. Put over the fire in boiling water, and, after cooking three or four minutes, drain, rinse in cold water, and put on to cook in boiling salted water to cover. Drain as soon as tender.

## How to Cut Gherkins for a Garnish.

Select small cucumber pickles of uniform size. With a sharp knife cut them, lengthwise, into slices thin as paper, without detaching the slices at one end; then spread out the slices as a fan is spread.

### How to Fringe Celery.

Cut the stalks into pieces about two inches in length. Beginning on the round side at one end, with a thin, sharp knife, cut down half an inch as many times as possible; then turn the stalk half-way around and cut in the opposite direction, thus dividing the end into shreds, or a fringe. If desired, cut the opposite end in the same manner. Set aside in a pan of ice water containing a slice of lemon.

### How to Shred Romaine and Straight Lettuce.

Wash the lettuce leaves carefully, without removing them from the stalk; shake in the open air, and they will dry very quickly; fold in the middle, crosswise, and cut through in the fold. Hold the two pieces, one above the other, close to the meat-board with the left hand, and with a sharp knife cut in narrow ribbons not more than a quarter of an inch wide.

### How to Keep Celery, Watercress, Lettuce, Etc.

Many green vegetables—celery in particular—discolor or rust, if allowed to stand longer than a few hours after being wet. When brought from the market they may be put aside, in a tightly closed pail, or in a paper bag, in a cool, dry place. By thus excluding the air they will keep fresh several days. A short time before serving put them into ice-cold water to which a slice or two of lemon has been added.

## How to Cook Sweetbreads and Brains.

Remove the thin outer skin or membrane and soak in cold water, changing the water often, an hour or more. Cover with salted boiling water, acidulated with lemon juice and flavored with vegetables, and cook, just below the boiling-point, twenty minutes. They are then ready for preparation in any of the ways mentioned. Tie the brains in a cloth before cooking.

## How to Pickle Nasturtium Seeds.

As the seeds are gathered wash and dry them; then put them into vinegar to which salt (half a teaspoonful to a pint) has been added. When a sufficient quantity has been collected, scald fresh vinegar, add salt as before, and the seeds from which the first vinegar has been drained. Pour scalding hot into bottles, having the seeds completely covered with vinegar.

## Nasturtium Vinegar.

Fill a quart jar loosely with nasturtium blossoms fully blown; add a shallot and one-third a clove of garlic, both finely chopped, half a red pepper, and cold cider vinegar to fill the jar; cover closely and set aside two months. Dissolve a teaspoonful of salt in the vinegar, then strain and filter.

## Tarragon Vinegar.

Fill a fruit jar with fresh tarragon leaves or shoots, putting them in loosely; add the thin *yellow* paring of half a lemon with two or three cloves, and fill the jar with white wine or cider vinegar. Screw down the cover tightly, and allow the jar to stand in the sun two weeks; strain the vinegar through a cloth, pressing out the liquid from the leaves; then pass through filter paper, and bottle for future use. If a quantity be prepared, it were better to seal the bottles.

## Fines Herbes Vinegar.

INGREDIENTS.

- 2 cups of tarragon vinegar.
- 2 tablespoonfuls of garden cress, chopped fine.
- 2 tablespoonfuls of sweet marjoram, chopped fine.
- 2 cloves of garlic, chopped fine.
- 4 small green capsicums, chopped fine.
- 2 shallots, chopped fine.

*Method.*—Mix the ingredients in a pint fruit jar, cover closely, and set in the sun; after two weeks strain, pass through filter paper and store in tightly corked bottles.

"The tender lettuce brings on softer sleep."—W. King, Art of Cookery.

## Fines Herbes Vinegar, No. 2.

INGREDIENTS.

- 1 pint of tarragon vinegar.
- 2 tablespoonfuls of seeds of garden cress, bruised or crushed.
- 2 tablespoonfuls of celery seeds, crushed.
- 2 tablespoonfuls of parsley seeds, crushed.
- 4 capsicums, chopped fine.
- 2 cloves of garlic, chopped fine.

*Method.*—Prepare as in preceding recipe.

## To Decorate Salads with Mayonnaise by Use of Pastry Bag and Tubes.

Make the dressing very thick by the addition of oil, or use "jelly mayonnaise." Put the dressing into a pastry bag with star tube attached; twist the large end of the bag with the left hand, pressing the mixture towards the tube, and with the right guide the tube as in writing, to produce the pattern desired. To form stars, hold the bag in an upright position, point downward, press out a little of the dressing, then push the tube down gently, and raise it quickly to break the flow.

# SALAD DRESSINGS.

"Just, as in nature, thy proportions be,
As full of concord their variety."

### French Dressing.

INGREDIENTS.

- ½ a teaspoonful of salt.
- A few grains of cayenne or paprica.
- ¼ a teaspoonful of pepper.
- 2 to 6 tablespoonfuls of vinegar or lemon juice.
- 6 tablespoonfuls of oil.

If desired,—

- ½ a teaspoonful of prepared mustard.
- ½ a teaspoonful of onion juice, or rub the salad-bowl with slice of onion, or clove of garlic.

*Method.*—Mix the condiments, add the oil and mix again; then add the acid, a few drops at a time, and beat until an emulsion is formed; then pour over the vegetables, toss with the spoon and fork, and serve. In Chicago a method has obtained that is well worth a trial: Put a bit of ice into the bowl with the condiments, and, by means of a fork pressed against or into this, use in mixing.

*Second Method.*—Pour the oil over the vegetables, toss, until the oil is evenly distributed, and dust with salt and pepper; then add the acid and toss again. When the salad is prepared at the table, the vegetables may be dressed in a bowl, then arranged on the serving-dish; or, if but one vegetable is used, it is preferable to serve from the dish in which it is dressed.

## To Mix a Quantity of Dressing.

Put all the ingredients into a fruit jar, fit on one or more rubbers and the cover; then shake the jar vigorously, until a smooth dressing is formed.

## Claret Dressing.

(*For lettuce or fruit salad.*)

Mix half a teaspoonful of salt, a dash of pepper, white or paprica, and four tablespoonfuls of oil; add gradually one tablespoonful of claret and one tablespoonful of lemon juice or vinegar.

## Mayonnaise Dressing.

INGREDIENTS.

- The yolks of 2 raw eggs.
- 1 pint of olive oil.
- 2 tablespoonfuls of vinegar.
- 2 tablespoonfuls of lemon juice.
- ½ a teaspoonful of salt.
- A few grains of cayenne or paprica.

If desired,—

- 1 teaspoonful, each, of mustard and powdered sugar.

*Method.*—An amateur will probably find it helpful to have all the utensils and ingredients thoroughly chilled, but the professional salad-maker thinks it expedient to have the ingredients and utensils of the same temperature as the room in which the dressing is to be served. Beat the yolks with a small wooden spoon or silver fork, add the condiments and mix again; then add one teaspoonful of vinegar, and, when well mixed with the other ingredients, add the oil, at first drop by drop. When the mixture has become of good consistency the oil may be added faster. When it is too thick to beat well, add a little of the lemon juice, then more oil, and so on alternately, until the ingredients are used. If a very heavy dressing is desired, as when it is to be put on with forcing-bag and tubes for a garnish, an additional half a cup of oil may be added without increasing the quantity of acid.

In preparing mayonnaise, there is absolutely no danger of curdling, if the eggs be fresh and the oil be added slowly, especially if the materials and utensils have been thoroughly chilled. If the yolks do not thicken when beaten with the condiments, but spread out over the bowl, you have sufficient indication that they will not thicken upon the addition of the oil, and it were better to select others and begin again. Take care to add the teaspoonful of acid to the yolks and condiments before beginning to drop in the oil, as this lessens the liability of the mixture to curdle.

## How to Make Mayonnaise in Quantity.

If four quarts or more of dressing be required, make the full amount at one time; cut down the number of yolks to one for each pint of oil, but keep the usual proportions of the other ingredients. Use a Dover egg-beater from the start; after a little a teaspoonful of oil can be added instead of drops, and, very soon, a much larger quantity.

## Curdled Mayonnaise.

Occasionally a mayonnaise will assume a curdled appearance; under such circumstances, often the addition of a very little of white of egg or a few drops of lemon juice, with thorough beating, will cause the sauce to resume its former smoothness. In case it does not become smooth, put the yolk of an egg into a cold bowl, beat well, and add to it the curdled mixture, a little at a time.

### Red Mayonnaise.

Mix a level teaspoonful of Italian tomato pulp with a teaspoonful of mayonnaise dressing, and when well blended beat very thoroughly into a cup or more of the dressing, or add dressing until the desired tint is attained.

### Red Mayonnaise, No. 2.

(*For fish.*)

Pound dried lobster coral in a mortar, sift, and add gradually to the dressing, to secure the shade desired. Or, after the salad is arranged in the bowl, or in nests, mask the top with mayonnaise of the usual color, and sift the coral over the centre, leaving a ring of yellow around the edge.

### Sauce Tartare.

Make a mayonnaise dressing, using tarragon vinegar. To each cup of dressing add one shallot, chopped fine, two tablespoonfuls, each, of finely chopped capers, olives and cucumber pickles, one tablespoonful of chopped parsley, and one-fourth a teaspoonful of powdered tarragon.

## Sardine Mayonnaise.

Skin and bone three sardines and pound them to a pulp; sift the cooked yolks of three eggs and add to the pulp; work until smooth, then add to one cup of mayonnaise dressing.

## Jelly Mayonnaise.

(*Used for masking cold fish or salads, or as a garnish with forcing-bag and tube.*)

To a cup of mayonnaise dressing beat in gradually from two tablespoonfuls to one-third a cup of chilled but liquid aspic. More seasoning may be needed. Apply to a cold surface, or chill before using with forcing-bag.

## Livournaise Sauce.

To a cup of mayonnaise dressing add a grating of nutmeg, one tablespoonful of chopped parsley and the pulp of eight anchovies.

To prepare the anchovies, wash, dry, remove skin and bones and pound to a pulp in a mortar.

## Boiled Dressing for Chicken Salad.

INGREDIENTS.

- ½ a cup of chicken stock, well reduced.
- ½ a cup of vinegar.
- ¼ a cup of mixed mustard.
- 1 teaspoonful of salt.
- ½ a teaspoonful of paprica.
- Yolks of 5 eggs.
- ½ a cup of oil.
- ½ a cup of thick, sweet cream.

*Method.*—Simmer the liquor in which a fowl has been cooked, until it is well reduced. Put the stock, vinegar and mustard into a double boiler, and add the salt and pepper. Beat the yolks of the eggs and add carefully to the hot mixture, cooking in the same manner as a boiled custard. When cold and ready to serve, beat in with a whisk the oil, and then fold in the cream, beaten stiff with a Dover egg-beater. Melted butter, added before the dressing is cold, may be substituted for the oil.

## Boiled Salad Dressing.

Ingredients.

- 1 teaspoonful of mustard.
- ½ a teaspoonful of salt.
- ¼ a teaspoonful of paprica.
- Yolks of 3 eggs.
- 4 tablespoonfuls of melted butter.
- 2 tablespoonfuls of vinegar.
- ½ a cup of thick cream.
- 2 tablespoonfuls of lemon juice.

*Method.*—Mix together the mustard, salt and paprica, and add the yolks of eggs; stir well and add slowly the butter, vinegar and lemon juice, and cook in the double boiler until thick as soft custard. When cool and ready to serve, add the cream, beaten stiff with the Dover egg-beater.

## Cream Salad Dressing.

Ingredients.

- ¾ a cup of thick cream.
- 2 tablespoonfuls of vinegar or lemon juice.
- ¼ a teaspoonful of salt.
- A dash of white pepper and paprica.

*Method.*—Add the seasonings to the cream and beat with a Dover egg-beater until smooth and light. Add a scant fourth a cup of grated horseradish, for a change. The radish should be freshly grated, and added to the cream after it is beaten.

## Dressing for Cole=Slaw.

Beat the yolks of three eggs with half a teaspoonful of made mustard, a dash of pepper and one-fourth a teaspoonful of salt; add one-third a cup of vinegar and two tablespoonfuls of butter, and cook over hot water until slightly thickened. Set aside to become cold before using.

## Bacon Sauce.

Heat five tablespoonfuls of bacon fat; cook in it two tablespoonfuls of flour and a dash of paprica; add five tablespoonfuls of vinegar and half a cup of water; stir until boiling; then beat in the beaten yolks of two eggs, and a little salt if necessary. Do not allow the sauce to boil after the eggs are added. Add to salad after it has become thoroughly cold. Good with dandelion, endive, chicory, corn salad or lettuce.

## Hollandaise Sauce.

Beat half a cup of butter to a cream; add the yolks of four eggs, one at a time, beating in each thoroughly; add one-fourth a teaspoonful of salt, a dash of paprica or cayenne, and half a cup of boiling water. Cook over hot water until thick, adding gradually the juice of half a lemon. Chill before using. This is good, especially for a fish salad, in the place of mayonnaise.

## Bernaise Sauce.

Use tarragon instead of plain vinegar, omit the water, with the exception of one tablespoonful, and the hollandaise becomes bernaise sauce. Oil may be used in the place of butter. The sauce resembles a firm mayonnaise, and, as it keeps its shape well, is particularly adapted for garnishing with pastry bag and tube.

**Cucumber Salad for Fish Course.**
(See page 36)

**Cooked Vegetable Salad**
(See page 37)

# VEGETABLE SALADS SERVED WITH FRENCH DRESSING.

"Bestrewed with lettuce and cool salad herbs."

## Lettuce Salad.

Wash and drain the lettuce leaves; toss lightly, so as to remove every drop of water. Sprinkle them with oil, a few drops at a time, tossing the leaves about with spoon and fork after each addition. When each leaf glistens with oil (there should be no oil in the bottom of the bowl) shake over them a few drops of vinegar, then dust with salt and freshly ground pepper. The cutting of lettuce is considered a culinary sin; but, when the straight-leaved lettuce, or the Romaine, is to be used, better effects, at least as far as appearance is concerned, will be produced, if the lettuce be cut into ribbons. To do this, wash the lettuce carefully, without removing the leaves from the stem; fold together across the centre, and with a sharp, thin knife cut into ribbons *less* than half an inch in width.

## Endive Salad.

Prepare as lettuce salad, first rubbing over the bowl with a clove of garlic cut in halves. A few sprigs of chives, chopped fine, are exceedingly palatable, sprinkled over a lettuce, endive, string-bean, or other bean salad.

## A Few Combinations.

Dress each vegetable separately with the dressing; then arrange upon the serving-dish. Or, have the salad arranged upon the serving-dish and pour the dressing over all; then toss together and serve. About three tablespoonfuls of oil, with other ingredients in accordance, will be needed for one pint of vegetable.

1. Lettuce, tomatoes cut in halves, sprinkled with powdered tarragon, and parsley or chives.

2. Lettuce, moulded spinach and fine-chopped beets.

3. Lettuce, Boston baked beans and chives.

4. Lettuce and peppergrass.

5. Lettuce, shredded sweet peppers or pimentos, and sliced pecan nuts or almonds.

6. Lettuce, tomatoes stuffed with peas or string beans cut small, and chives chopped fine.

7. Lettuce, asparagus tips and sliced radishes. Arrange the lettuce at the edge of dish, inside a ring of radishes sliced thin, without removing the red skins; centre of asparagus tips, with radish cut to resemble a flower.

8. Lettuce, shredded tomatoes and shredded green peppers.

9. Shredded lettuce, English walnuts, and almonds or cooked chestnuts, sliced.

10. Lettuce, Neufchatel cheese in slices and shredded pimentos.

11. Lettuce, cauliflower, string beans and shredded pimentos.

12. Lettuce or cress, artichoke slices and powdered tarragon.

13. Shredded cabbage and shredded green peppers.

14. Cauliflower broken into flowerets, string beans cut into small pieces, and beets cut in fancy shapes or chopped. Arrange each vegetable in a mass by itself; surround with lettuce.

15. Cucumbers and new onions, sliced.

16. Watercress, diced boiled beets, and olives in centre.

17. Lettuce, Brussels sprouts and chopped pepper.

## Lentil Salad.

Soak the lentils over night; wash and rinse thoroughly, then cook until tender, adding hot water as needed. Drain, and when cold mix with each pint of lentils about five tablespoonfuls of oil, two tablespoonfuls of tarragon vinegar and one teaspoonful, each, of capers, parsley, chives and cucumber pickles, all, save the capers, chopped fine. Serve in a mound, on a bed of lettuce leaves. Garnish with heart leaves of lettuce at the top and sections of tomato, or diamonds of tomato jelly, at the base.

**Potato Balls, Pecan Meats, and Cress Salad.**

**Potato-and-Nasturtium Salad.**
See page 34

## White=Bean Salad.

Toss one pint of white beans, cooked, with one tablespoonful of vinegar and three tablespoonfuls of oil, a little salt and a dash of cayenne or paprica. Arrange in a mound on a bed of shredded lettuce, and sprinkle with chives, parsley and pimentos, all finely chopped. Finish the top of the salad with a large pim-ola.

## Potato Salad.

(Miss Cohen.)

Ingredients.

- 3 cups of cold boiled potatoes, cut in cubes.
- 1 cup of pecan nuts, broken in pieces.
- 5 tablespoonfuls of oil.
- 1 tablespoonful of salt.
- ½ a teaspoonful of onion juice.
- A dash of cayenne.
- 2 or 3 tablespoonfuls of vinegar.
- Watercress.

*Method.*—Mix the potatoes and nuts, add the oil and mix again; add the other seasonings, and, when well mixed, set aside in a cool place an hour or more. Remove the coarse stalks from two bunches of watercress that have been well washed and dried. Season with French dressing and arrange in a wreath about the edge of the salad.

## Potato Salad.

(CARRIE M. DEARBORN.)

INGREDIENTS.

- 12 cold boiled potatoes.
- 4 cooked eggs.
- 2 small Bermuda onions.
- Chopped parsley.
- 1 saltspoonful of white pepper.
- 2 teaspoonfuls of salt.
- 6 tablespoonfuls, each, of oil and vinegar.
- ½ a teaspoonful of powdered sugar.

*Method.*—Cut the potatoes into dice and chop the eggs fine. Chop the onions, or slice them very thin. Sprinkle the potatoes, eggs and onions with the salt and pepper, and mix thoroughly. Pour the oil gradually over the mixture, stirring and tossing continually; lastly, mix with the other ingredients the vinegar, in which the sugar has been dissolved. Sprinkle chopped parsley over the top.

## Potato Salad.

INGREDIENTS.

- 1 quart of cubes of cold boiled potatoes.
- 1½ teaspoonfuls of salt.
- ¼ a teaspoonful of paprica.
- 3 tablespoonfuls of vinegar.
- 4 tablespoonfuls of oil.
- Capers, beets, whites and yolks of eggs, and lettuce.

*Method.*—To the potato cubes add the salt, pepper and oil, and mix thoroughly; add the vinegar and mix again. Pile the cubes in a mound in the salad-bowl. Mark out the surface of the mound into quarters with capers; fill in two opposite sections with chopped beet; use chopped whites of eggs in a third, and sifted yolks of eggs in the fourth section. Finish with a border of parsley.

## Potato=and=Nasturtium Salad.

(E. J. McKenzie.)

Ingredients.

- 1 quart of potatoes, cut in cubes.
- ½ a cup of chopped gherkins.
- 1 cup of tender nasturtium shoots, cut in bits.
- 2 tablespoonfuls of pickled nasturtium seeds.
- Onion juice or garlic.
- 6 tablespoonfuls of oil.
- 5 tablespoonfuls of vinegar.
- Salt and pepper.
- Chopped parsley.

*Method.*—Mix the potatoes, gherkins, nasturtium shoots and seeds in a bowl rubbed over with garlic; add the oil, vinegar and seasonings, and mix again. Pile in a mound on a serving-dish, dust with chopped parsley, and garnish with a wreath of nasturtium blossoms and leaves.

## Stuffed Beets.

Boil new beets, of even size, until tender. Set aside for some hours, or over night, covered with vinegar. When ready to serve, rub off the skin, scoop out the centre of each to form a cup, and arrange the cups on lettuce leaves. For each five cups chop fine a cucumber. Make a French dressing of two tablespoonfuls of oil, half a tablespoonful (scant) of vinegar, one-fourth a teaspoonful, each, of paprica and salt. Stir the dressing into the cucumber and fill the beets with the mixture. Of the beet removed to form the cups, cut slices and stamp out from these stars or other fanciful shapes, and use to decorate the top of each cup.

Chopped radish, cress, olives or celery are all admissible for a filling.

## Salad of Brussels Sprouts and Beets.

Soak the sprouts in salted water; then drain and cook in salted boiling water about fifteen minutes, or until tender; drain and cool. Dress with French dressing and pile in a mound. Finish the top with a fanciful-shaped figure cut from a slice of pickled beet, and place a wreath of cooked beet, chopped and seasoned with French dressing, about the whole.

## Macedoine Salad.

Cut pieces of carrot and turnip one inch long and half an inch thick. Put over the fire in boiling water and bring quickly to the boiling-point; drain, cover with fresh water, and cook until tender; score the top of each piece and insert an asparagus point. Dip the pieces in a little melted gelatine and set alternately in a circle on the serving-dish. Have carrots cut in small cubes or straws, turnips and beet root the same, green string beans cut in small pieces, asparagus and peas, all cooked separately until tender. Mix with French dressing and dispose inside the circle. Each vegetable may be massed by itself, or all may be mixed together. Finish the top with half a dozen short stalks of asparagus.

## Tomato=and=Onion Salad.

Peel and shred four tomatoes; slice thinly a very mild onion and separate into rings; dress freely with oil and tarragon vinegar, and season with salt and pepper. Serve on lettuce leaves, sprinkling the whole with fine-chopped parsley and green peppers.

### Endive,=Tomato=and=Green=String=Bean Salad.

Dress the well-blanched stalks of a head of endive, three tomatoes, peeled, cut in halves and chilled, and a cup of cold cooked string beans, separately, with French dressing, using in the dressing tarragon vinegar and a few drops of onion juice; then arrange on a serving-dish.

**Endive, Tomato, and Green String Bean Salad.**

**Stuffed Beets.**
See page 34

## Cucumber Salad.

*(German style.)*

Pare large cucumbers and cut them into thin slices; cut each slice round and round so as to form a long, narrow curling strip. Let these strips stand two hours in salted ice water, drain, and dry in a soft cloth. Serve with French dressing. Toss first in the oil, then add the condiments, and lastly the vinegar. Americans would prefer to omit the salt from the ice water, as it softens the cucumber.

## Cucumber Salad for Fish Course.

With a handy slicer remove the outside rind from the cucumbers, cut in thin slices, and let stand in ice-water to chill. Wipe dry, and arrange the slices in the salad bowl in the form of a Greek cross. Make a French dressing, in the proportion of three tablespoonfuls of cider vinegar to six tablespoonfuls of oil, half a teaspoonful of salt, and a dash of paprica. Rub the inside of the salad bowl with the cut side of an onion before the salad is disposed in it.

## Cooked Vegetable Salad.

Dress cooked kidney beans, peas, and balls cut from potatoes, each separately with French dressing, to which a few drops of onion juice have been added. Dispose upon a serving-dish and let stand in a cool place an hour or more. Garnish at serving with heart leaves of lettuce.

# Potato Salad.

(*German Style.*)

I<small>NGREDIENTS</small>.

- 1 quart of potato slices or cubes.
- About ½ a cup of beef broth.
- 1 teaspoonful of salt.
- ½ a teaspoonful of paprica.
- 8 tablespoonfuls of oil.
- 1 tablespoonful of grated onion.
- 2 hard boiled eggs.
- 4 tablespoonfuls of vinegar.
- 1 teaspoonful of mustard.
- 1 teaspoonful of sugar.
- Fine chopped parsley.
- (1 cup of mushrooms.)

*Method.*—Boil the potatoes without paring. German potatoes, which are waxy rather than mealy, may be procured in large cities especially for salads. Peel the potatoes and cut them while hot into slices or cubes; pour over them as much beef broth as they will readily absorb and sprinkle with the salt and pepper, the oil and onion; mix lightly and set aside for some hours. Then add the whites of the eggs chopped fine, the yolks passed through a sieve, and mix with the rest of the oil, stirred with the vinegar into the mustard and sugar. After disposing in the dish, sprinkle with the parsley. If mushrooms be at hand, simmer ten or fifteen minutes in broth, break in pieces, and add to the salad with the egg.

# SALADS, LARGELY VEGETABLE, SERVED WITH MAYONNAISE, CREAM OR BOILED DRESSING.

### Cauliflower Salad.

Soak the cauliflower in salted water an hour; cook in boiling salted water until tender; drain and chill, then sprinkle with French dressing and set aside for half an hour. Sever the flowerets partly from the stalk, but so as not to change their relative positions, and place on a serving-dish; put heart leaves of lettuce between the flowerets and about the base of the vegetable; pour a cup of mayonnaise dressing over the whole, and sprinkle with pimentos or fine-chopped parsley. In serving, separate the flowerets with a sharp knife.

### Tomatoes Stuffed with Nuts and Celery.

Peel the tomatoes; cut out a circular piece at the stem end of each and scoop out the flesh so as to form cups. Chill thoroughly, then fill with English walnut or pecan meats, broken into pieces, and celery, cut into small pieces and mixed with mayonnaise. Serve on lettuce leaves.

### Stuffed=Tomato Salad.

Ingredients.

- 6 smooth, small-sized tomatoes.
- 6 tablespoonfuls of chicken, veal or tongue, cut fine.
- 6 tablespoonfuls of peas.
- 3 olives, chopped fine.
- 3 gherkins, chopped fine.
- 2 tablespoonfuls of capers.
- Salt and pepper.
- Mayonnaise dressing.

*Method.*—Remove a round piece from the stem end of the tomatoes and scoop out the seeds and centre. Chill thoroughly. When ready to serve, mix together the solid part removed from the tomatoes, cut fine, and the other ingredients; season to taste with salt and pepper, adding also mayonnaise to hold the mixture together. With this fill the tomatoes, put them in nests of lettuce or cress, and force a star of mayonnaise on the top of each tomato.

### Tomato Salad, Horseradish Dressing.

Plunge the tomatoes, placed in a wire basket, into a kettle of hot water; remove at once and rub off the skin; chill thoroughly and cut in halves. Serve on lettuce leaves with a star of cream dressing, seasoned with grated horseradish, on the top of each slice.

### Tomato=and=Sweetbread Salad.

Cook two sweetbreads as directed on another page, or braise with vegetables. Cool between two plates bearing a weight. When cold cut into slices and stamp into rounds of suitable size to use with slices of tomato. Cover the slices of sweetbread with chaud-froid sauce and decorate with fine-chopped parsley or sifted yolk of egg; pour over a little melted aspic. When the aspic is set, trim neatly, and arrange each round of sweetbread on a slice of chilled tomato. Serve inside a border of lettuce around a salad made of the trimmings of the sweetbreads and a cucumber cut in cubes and dressed with mayonnaise.

**Cress, Cucumber, and Tomato Salad.**
See page 41

**Tomato Jelly with Celery and Nuts.**
See page 43

## Cress,=Cucumber=and=Tomato Salad.

Wash the cress and shake dry; arrange as a bed on a serving-dish, discarding the coarse stems; above this make a smaller bed of cucumbers, cut in slices or dice and dressed with French dressing, using three tablespoonfuls of oil and one of vinegar or lemon juice to a pint of cucumber. Arrange peeled tomatoes, chilled and cut in pieces, upon the cucumbers. Serve with French, cream or mayonnaise dressing.

## Tomatoes Stuffed with Cucumber.

Peel five tomatoes, cut off the stem ends and scoop out the pulp, thus forming cups; set, turned upside down, in a cool place. Chop fine the solid pulp from the tomatoes and one cucumber, chilled before chopping; stir into a cup of cream dressing and fill the tomatoes with the mixture. Salt and pepper will be needed in addition to that in the dressing. If at hand, a pimento may be chopped with the other ingredients, or two tablespoonfuls of grated horseradish may be used. Serve at once on lettuce leaves.

## Tomatoes Stuffed with Jelly.

Chop one sweetbread and one cucumber fine. To each cup (solid and liquid) add one-fourth a teaspoonful, each, of salt and paprica, a few drops of onion juice and a tablespoonful of capers; add also half a tablespoonful of granulated gelatine, soaked in two or three tablespoonfuls of cold water and melted over hot water. Stir until the mixture begins to congeal, then fill into tomatoes prepared as above. Set aside on the ice for half an hour, at least; then serve on lettuce leaves with either mayonnaise, boiled or cream dressing. Calf's brains, chicken, veal, tongue or ham may be substituted for the sweetbread.

## Tomatoes Farces à l'Aspic.

### Ingredients.

- 6 even-sized ripe tomatoes.
- 1 pint of aspic jelly.
- ½ a cup of lobster meat, chopped fine.
- 1 tablespoonful of capers.
- 2 yolks of hard-boiled eggs.
- Mayonnaise, parsley, lettuce.

*Method.*—Scoop out the centres of the tomatoes, after removing the skin, and chill thoroughly. Pass the yolks through a sieve, add to the lobster, with the capers, half a cup of mayonnaise and half a cup of chicken aspic, thick and cold, but not set; stir these in a dish standing in ice water until nearly set; then fill the cavities in the tomatoes with the mixture. Brush over the outside of the tomatoes with half-set aspic; when the aspic is set, repeat twice, then set aside on ice for some time before serving. Serve on a bed of lettuce seasoned with French dressing. Garnish each tomato with a sprig of parsley and the salad-dish with blocks of aspic. Anchovies or any cooked fish may be substituted for the lobster. Serve with mayonnaise.

## Tomato Jelly.

Soak three-fourths a box of gelatine in half a cup of cold water. Cook a can of tomatoes, half an onion, a stalk of celery, a bay leaf, two cloves, a teaspoonful of salt and a dash of paprica ten minutes. Add two tablespoonfuls of tarragon vinegar and the gelatine, stir till dissolved, strain, and mould in a ring mould. When cold turn from the mould and fill the centre with

## CELERY=AND=NUT SALAD.

Cut fine tender stalks of celery and English walnuts and mix with French dressing. Garnish the centre of the salad and the border of the jelly with tender leaves of lettuce and bits of curled celery.

## Tomato=Jelly Salad, No. 2.

Make the jelly and mould as before. Fill in the centre of the ring with shredded cabbage, pimentos and pecan nuts, mixed with boiled dressing.

## Tomato Jelly with String Beans.

Cook tiny string beans until tender in boiling salted water; season while hot with onion juice, salt, pepper and tarragon vinegar. When cold add oil and toss the beans about until each bean is coated with the oil. Fill the centre of the jelly, fashioned in a ring mould, with the beans, and sprinkle over them a fine-chopped pimento. Garnish with lettuce leaves. Fine-chopped chives may be used in the place of the onion juice; they are particularly appropriate in any bean salad. If the beans are large, cut in halves lengthwise and the halves crosswise.

Tomato jelly may be served in a ring mould with turkey, oyster, plain chicken, French chicken, and other salads. The oysters should be scalded and drained, then marinated with French dressing. Chicken and turkey should also be marinated before mixing with celery and the mayonnaise or boiled dressing.


## Tomato=and=Artichoke Salad.

(MRS. E. M. LUCAS, IN BOSTON COOKING-SCHOOL MAGAZINE.)

Choose medium-sized tomatoes, firm and smooth skinned. Peel them, cut a slice from the stem end and remove the seeds with a small spoon. Sprinkle the interior of these cups with salt and set on ice. When ready to serve, wipe them dry and fill with artichokes cut into dice and mixed with mayonnaise. Serve on lettuce leaves. Use tarragon vinegar in preparing the dressing. Cook the artichoke hearts until just tender,—no longer,—in salted boiling water, then drain and cool.


## Artichoke Salad.

(*For game.*)

(Mrs. E. M. Lucas, in Boston Cooking-School Magazine.)

Peel three oranges, remove the pith and white skin and slice lengthwise; use an equal amount of tender blanched celery stalks cut into inch lengths. Mix together lightly with two tablespoonfuls of olive oil, one tablespoonful of lemon juice, half a teaspoonful of salt and a quarter a teaspoonful of paprica. Heap together lightly on a serving-dish and surround with cooked hearts of artichokes cut into quarters; wreathe with blanched celery leaves.

## Artichoke Salad.

(*Used as a border for shrimp, lobster, chicken and other salads.*)

(Mrs. E. M. Lucas, in Boston Cooking-School Magazine.)

Cut boiled artichokes into quarter-inch slices and stamp out with a French vegetable cutter. To half a pint add one tablespoonful of olive oil, half a tablespoonful of tarragon vinegar and one-fourth a teaspoonful of salt; toss lightly together and let stand one hour; drain, and arrange as a border with an outer layer of tiny blanched lettuce leaves.

2. Scoop out the centres of the artichokes and fill with mayonnaise, or with ravigote, tartare or tyrolienne sauce. Serve on lettuce leaves as a border to a meat or fish salad.

3. Fill the centres with walnut meats, sliced, or tender celery stalks, cut fine and mixed with mayonnaise.

## Asparagus Salad.

Cut cold cooked asparagus into pieces an inch long, mix lightly with cream dressing and serve, in individual portions, on curly lettuce leaves.

## Asparagus=and=Salmon Salad.

Mix cold cooked salmon with mayonnaise, form in a mound and encircle with a wreath of cold cooked asparagus tips dressed with French dressing.

## Asparagus=and=Cauliflower Salad.

Break the cooked cauliflower into its flowerets, dispose in the centre of the serving-dish and surround with a wreath of cooked asparagus tips. Pour over the whole a mayonnaise, a boiled or a cream dressing, and sprinkle with chopped capers or pimentos.

## Salad of Turnips with Asparagus Tips.

Cook the turnips in boiling salted water until tender; drain, and cut out the centres, forming cups. Sprinkle the inside with oil and a few grains of salt, and, when the oil is absorbed, pour over the cups a little lemon juice or vinegar. Set aside to become cool. When ready to serve, arrange the cups on shredded lettuce and fill with cooked asparagus tips, cold and mixed with mayonnaise or French dressing, as desired. Peas, flageolets or wax beans, cut fine, may be used instead of the asparagus. Garnish with radishes.

## Green=Pea Salad.

Mix the peas with a cream dressing; serve in nests of lettuce; garnish the top of each nest with a little chopped beet, or a fanciful figure cut from a pickled beet or pimento.

## Green=Pea=and=Potato Salad.

Mix equal parts of cold cooked peas and potatoes cut in very small cubes; season with salt and pepper, and serve as green-pea salad.

## Asparagus Salad.

Scrape the scales from the stalks, and cook, standing upright in boiling salted water, until tender; drain and chill thoroughly. Serve on lettuce leaves with French dressing. Garnish the lettuce with hard-boiled eggs cut in quarters lengthwise.

## Macedoine of Vegetable Salad.

Dress one cup, each, of cooked carrots and turnips, cut in dice, string beans, cut small, green peas, and half a cup of cooked beets, cut small, with French dressing; add two tablespoonfuls of chopped gherkins; drain, and mix with sufficient jelly mayonnaise to hold the vegetables together. Arrange in dome shape and cover with more jelly mayonnaise. Set a row of sliced gherkins near the top, and fill in the space to the top with string beans or asparagus tips. Surround the base with alternate rounds of beet and potato overlapping one another. Decorate the space above with slices of potato and beet cut in diamonds, and surround the base with light-green aspic cut in diamonds. One pint of aspic will be sufficient; use chicken stock, and tint with color paste.

## Russian Vegetable Salad.

Select two moulds of suitable shape and size (tin basins or earthen bowls will do) and chill in ice water. Have ready cooked balls, cut from carrots and turnips, and cooked string beans and cauliflower, all marinated with French dressing. Drain the vegetables, dip them into half-set aspic, and arrange against the chilled sides of the moulds; then fill the moulds with aspic jelly. When set, with a hot spoon scoop out the aspic from the centre of each mould and fill in the space with a mixture of the vegetables and jelly mayonnaise, leaving an open space at the top to be filled with half-set aspic. When thoroughly chilled and set, turn from the moulds, the smaller mould above the other. Garnish with flowerets of cauliflower, dipped in aspic and chilled, and lettuce. Serve with mayonnaise.

**Russian Vegetable Salad.**

**Macedoine of Vegetable Salad.**
See page 47

### Stuffed=Cucumber Salad.

Pare a short cucumber and cut it lengthwise in two parts; remove the seeds and let chill in ice water for an hour. Chop together the solid part of a peeled and seeded tomato, half a slice of new onion, a stalk of celery and a sprig of parsley; mix with mayonnaise or a boiled dressing and use as a filling for the well-dried halves of cucumber. Serve on cress or lettuce.

### Cowslip=and=Cream=Cheese Salad.

(See cut facing page 58.)

Cook the cowslip leaves until tender in boiling salted water, reserving a few choice leaves with blossoms for a garnish. Chop fine, season to taste with salt and paprica, press into a mould, and set aside to become chilled. Slice chilled cream cheese (Neufchatel or cottage) in uniform slices, and arrange at the sides of the mound. Serve with French or mayonnaise dressing.

### Cauliflower Salad, Egg Garnish.

Separate a cauliflower into flowerets and boil in salted water until tender, *not longer*. Drain carefully. Season with oil, vinegar, salt, pepper, and a sprinkling of chopped tarragon leaves (or use tarragon vinegar). Arrange symmetrically in an earthen bowl, having the upper surface level. Let stand to become thoroughly chilled, then turn on to a serving-dish; the shape of the mould will be retained. Cover with mayonnaise dressing or Sauce Tartare, and surround with lengthwise quarters of hard-boiled eggs.

### Potato Salad with Mayonnaise.

Boil the potatoes and let cool without paring. Then remove the skins and cut into slices, balls, or cubes. Squeeze over them a little onion juice, sprinkle with fine-chopped parsley, and let stand in a French dressing several hours. Mix the dressing after the usual formula, and use enough to moisten well the potato. When ready to serve, make nests of heart leaves of lettuce, put a spoonful of the potato in each, with a teaspoonful of mayonnaise above, sprinkle the mayonnaise with capers, and press the quarter of a hard-boiled egg into the top of the mayonnaise. Or add the chopped white of egg to the potato before marinating, and sift the yolk over the mayonnaise.

# FISH SALADS.

Ever, and justly, fish have taken high rank in the list of salad ingredients. No wonder, when we consider that nothing excels in delicacy of flavor many a variety of fish; and, while fish are not necessarily expensive in any locality, in many sections of the country their cost is merely nominal. Then, too, salad-making appeals largely to one's artistic nature, and the products of sea and fresh water are constantly furnishing opportunities for studies in many and varied shades of color. The lobster's vivid red, the brilliant tints of the salmon and red snapper, the delicate pink of shrimps, the dull white of scallops and halibut, and the bluish gray of mackerel and bluefish, each, in its season, may be made to contrast most effectively with fresh green herbs and yellow dressings.

Oysters, scallops and little-neck clams are frequently served in salads without cooking. These should be carefully washed, then drained and set aside in a marinade for an hour. When cooked, they should be heated to the boiling-point in their own liquor, then drained and cut in halves. The adductor muscle of the oyster—the white, button-shaped part that connects the animal with its shell—is often discarded. Other fish than shellfish, when used in salads, are boiled, broiled or baked; they present the best appearance, however, when boiled. Thudichum recommends sea water, whenever it is available, for boiling fish; lacking this, hot water, salted (an ounce of salt to a quart of water), and acidulated pleasantly with lemon juice or vinegar, is the proper medium of cooking. The addition of a slice or two of onion and carrot, a sprig of parsley, a stalk of celery, with aromatic herbs or spices, provided they be not used so freely as to overpower the delicate savor of the fish, is thought to improve the dish.

The quantity of water should be adjusted to the size of the fish; in no case should it be larger than will suffice to produce the desired result. At the moment the fish is immersed in the water the temperature should be at the boiling-point, and thereafter the vessel should be permitted to simmer during the process of cooking.

The fish may be cooked whole, or cut into small pieces, similar in shape and size. In the latter case a wire basket is of service, as, by this means, the fish may be easily removed from the water and drained. If the fish is to be served whole, remove the skin and fins, and, when thoroughly cold, mask with jelly mayonnaise or with a fancy butter. After chilling again, the mask may be decorated with capers, olives, eggs, etc. If the fish is to be used in flakes, the flakes will separate more easily while the fish is still hot. In marinating fish, let the proportions of oil and acid vary with the kind of fish; *i.e.*, according to the oily nature of the flesh.

# RECIPES.

### Brook=Trout Salad.

Dress the trout without removing the heads; boil as previously indicated. Remove the backbone without destroying the shape of the fish. Serve, thoroughly chilled, on crisp lettuce leaves dressed with claret or French dressing. Prepare the latter with tarragon vinegar.

### Brook Trout Moulded in Aspic.

Pour a little chicken aspic into a pickle or other dish of suitable shape and size for a single fish; when nearly set, lay a trout, prepared as above, upon the aspic, add a few spoonfuls of aspic, let it harden so that the fish may become fixed in place, then add aspic to cover. Slices of cucumber pickles, capers, or other ornaments, may be used. When the aspic is thoroughly set and chilled, remove from the mould and serve on two lettuce leaves, with any dressing desired.

### Halibut Salad.

Flake the fish and marinate with French dressing (three tablespoonfuls of oil, one tablespoonful of lemon juice or vinegar, a dash of salt and pepper, for each pint of fish); drain, and add half as much boiled potato, cut in small cubes and dressed with French dressing. Serve on a bed of lettuce leaves. Garnish with sardine dressing. Shredded lettuce or peas may be used in place of the potato.

# Halibut=and=Cucumber Salad.

### INGREDIENTS.

- 1 pound of cooked halibut.
- 2 tablespoonfuls of oil.
- 1 tablespoonful of lemon juice.
- A few drops of onion juice.
- Salt and pepper.
- 2 pimentos.
- Lettuce.
- Cucumbers.
- French dressing.

*Method.*—Flake one pound of cooked halibut while hot, and marinate with the oil, lemon juice, onion juice, salt and pepper. When cold drain and mix with the pimentos, shredded, after cutting from the same a few star-shaped or other fanciful figures. Arrange heart leaves of lettuce in an upright position in the centre of a serving-dish, the fish and pimentos around the lettuce, and, around these, one large or two small cucumbers, cut in small cubes and mixed with French dressing. With salmon use capers instead of pimentos. Use enough dressing to moisten the cucumbers thoroughly.

# Halibut Salad.

Steam a thick slice of chicken halibut, until the flesh separates easily from the bone. Remove the skin and bones without disturbing the shape of the fish. Marinate, while hot, with three tablespoonfuls of oil, one tablespoonful of vinegar or lemon juice, and salt and pepper. When cold put the fish on a serving-dish, and, using endive or Boston Market lettuce, put the ends of the leaves beneath the fish, so that the tops of the leaves will fall over upon the fish. Garnish the top with stars of mayonnaise. Between the leaves dispose sliced pim-olas and fans cut from small gherkins. Serve mayonnaise with the salad.

## Fillets of Halibut in Aspic, with Cucumber=and=Radish Salad.

Ingredients.

- 2 slices of halibut, cut half an inch or less in thickness.
- 1 lobster (a pound and a half).
- 3 tablespoonfuls of butter.
- ¼ a cup of flour.
- ¼ a cup of cream.
- ¼ a cup of stock.
- A dash of paprica.
- 1 tablespoonful of lemon juice.
- 1 teaspoonful of chopped parsley.
- ¼ a tablespoonful of salt.
- 1 quart of aspic.
- Olives.
- A bunch of radishes.
- 2 cucumbers.
- French dressing.

*Method.*—Remove the skin and bone from the halibut, thus securing eight fillets. Season with salt, pepper, onion and lemon juice. Chop the lobster meat fine; melt the butter, cook in it the flour and seasonings, add the cream and lobster stock, and, when cooked, stir in the chopped lobster. When cool spread upon one side of the fillets, roll up the fillets and fasten with wooden toothpicks that have been dipped in melted butter. Bake on a fish-sheet about fifteen minutes, basting with butter melted in hot water.

Set a plain border-mould in ice water; decorate the bottom and sides with pim-olas or gherkins cut in slices and dipped in half-set aspic; cover the decoration on the bottom with aspic, and, when set and the decorations on the side are "fixed" in place, arrange on the aspic the cold fillets of fish and fill the mould with more aspic. When cold turn from the mould and fill the centre with diced cucumbers and sliced radishes dressed with French dressing. Pass mayonnaise or French dressing in a separate dish. Surround the aspic with shredded lettuce if desired.

### Fillets of Halibut in Aspic with Cole=Slaw.

Use a generous half-pint of oysters in the place of the lobster, parboiling and draining before chopping, and fill in the centre of the aspic with coleslaw.

**Miroton of Fish and Potato Salad.**

**Cowslip and Cream Cheese Salad.**
See page 49

### Miroton of Fish and Potato.

Marinate one pint of cold cooked fish—salmon, cod, haddock, halibut, etc.—with three or four tablespoonfuls of oil, half a teaspoonful of salt, a dash of pepper and two tablespoonfuls of lemon juice. Marinate, separately, one pint of cold potatoes, cooked in their skins and cut in cubes, with the same quantity of dressing, adding also one teaspoonful of onion juice. Let stand in a cool place one hour or more. Have ready six hard-boiled eggs; cut a thin slice from the round end of each egg, that it may stand upright, then cut in quarters lengthwise. Dip into a little aspic jelly or melted gelatine and arrange the quarters in the form of a circle, with the yolks outside. Toss together the fish, potato and three tablespoonfuls of capers, and fill in the centre of the circle. Dust with fine-chopped parsley or beets; add a tuft of lettuce at the top and a few heart leaves of lettuce above the crown of eggs.

## Fish Salad Moulded in Aspic.

Cover the bottom of a mould with aspic to the depth of one-fourth an inch. Set the mould in ice water, and, when the aspic is set, arrange upon it a decoration of cooked vegetables cut in shapes with French cutter, or fashion a conventional design or some flower. Dogwood blossoms provide a simple pattern, and one easily carried out. Cut the four petals from a thin slice of cooked turnip and the centre of the blossom from carrot or lemon peel. Fasten each piece in place with liquid jelly, and, when set, cover with more jelly. To decorate the sides of the mould, take the figures on the point of a skewer, dip in jelly, then set in position against the *chilled* sides of the mould, and they will remain in place. After the jelly covering the figures on the bottom of the mould has "set," place a smaller mould in the centre of the aspic in the first, and fill this with ice and water. Pour in aspic to fill the space about the smaller mould, and, when this aspic is firm, dip out the water and ice. Fill with *warm* water and quickly remove the mould. Separate a pound of cooked fish into flakes, add half a cup of cold cooked peas, three or four gherkins, cut very fine, and three tablespoonfuls of capers. Mix together and then mix with one cup of mayonnaise made with jelly; with this fill the vacant space in the mould. When ready to serve, dip the mould very quickly into warm water, letting the water rise to the top of the mould, and invert over a serving-dish; remove the mould, and garnish with lettuce, tiny gherkins cut to resemble fans, blocks of aspic, or aspic moulded in shells, and mayonnaise.

## Fish Salad Moulded in Aspic, No. 2.

Decorate the mould as before; then put in a layer of the fish and dressing; when set, add a layer of aspic; alternate the layers until the materials are used or the mould is filled. Individual moulds may be prepared in the same way.

## Salad of Mackerel or Bluefish.

Separate a cooked fish into flakes and mix with the chopped whites and sifted yolks of three hard-boiled eggs. Season with French dressing, mix lightly and turn on to a bed of lettuce or cress, also seasoned with the dressing. Garnish with fans cut from small gherkins, or with pickled beet cut in fanciful shape or chopped.

## Salad of Salt Mackerel.

Freshen the fish carefully before cooking. Use equal parts of fish, flaked, and cold boiled potatoes. If potatoes are specially prepared for the purpose, cut them in cubes or balls, blanch, and cook in well-seasoned beef stock; drain, and add, when cold, to the fish. Season with French dressing. Arrange on a bed of cress and sift the yolk of an egg over the whole.

## Salad of Shad Roe and Cucumber.

Cook two shad roes with an onion, sliced, and a bay leaf, in salted, acidulated water twenty minutes; drain, and marinate with about two tablespoonfuls of oil, one tablespoonful of lemon juice and a dash of pepper and salt. When cold cut in small cubes. Rub the salad-bowl with a clove of garlic cut in halves. Cut a thoroughly chilled cucumber in dice; put the cucumber on a bed of lettuce leaves in the bottom of the bowl, and the roe, well drained, above; mask with mayonnaise,—nearly a cup will be required,—in the top insert a few heart leaves of lettuce, and place around the centre of the mound a circle of cucumber slices overlapping one another; or alternate these with lozenges cut from pickled beet.

### Boudins=de=Saumon Salad.

Butter four small dariole moulds, or small cups; sprinkle the butter with chopped parsley. Select four small pieces of cooked salmon, dry on a soft cloth so as to remove all oily liquor, and put a piece in each mould. Beat two eggs (or, better, one egg and the yolks of two) slightly, season with one-fourth a teaspoonful of salt, a dash of paprika and a few drops of anchovy essence or onion juice; add half a cup of milk, and, when well mixed, pour into the moulds around the fish. Set the moulds in a pan of hot water and bake until the custard is set. Do not let the water boil. Chill thoroughly, then turn from the moulds on to lettuce leaves. Serve with a star of mayonnaise dressing on the top of each *boudin*.

**Russian Salad.**

**Halibut Salad.**

**Russian Salad.**

(BOSTON COOKING-SCHOOL.)

INGREDIENTS.

- 1 cup of carrots.
- 1 cup of potatoes.
- 1 cup of peas.
- 1 cup of beans (flageolets preferred).
- 6 tablespoonfuls of oil.
- 3 tablespoonfuls of vinegar.
- 1 teaspoonful of salt.
- ¼ a teaspoonful of pepper.
- A head of lettuce.
- 1 cup of mayonnaise.
- 1 cup of shrimps.
- ¼ a lb. of smoked salmon.
- 1 hard-boiled egg.

*Method.*—Marinate the carrots and potatoes, cut in small pieces, also the peas and beans, with French dressing. Arrange on a dish in four sections, having lettuce for the foundation of each. Cover each vegetable with mayonnaise. Strew the tops of two sections with small pieces of smoked salmon; on a third section strew the sifted yolk of the egg, and on the fourth, the white of the egg, cut rather coarsely. Outline the inner side of each section with shrimps, by lightly pressing the ends of the shrimps into the mayonnaise. Finish with a tuft of lettuce in the centre of the dish.

## Spanish Salad.

In the centre of a flat serving-dish arrange a mound of endive. Peel tomatoes, divide into sections or cut in slices, and arrange these around the endive. Shell cold, hard-boiled eggs; cut in halves, crosswise, and in points; remove the yolks and pound to a paste with an equal amount of the flesh of lobster, shrimp, anchovies or salmon. With this paste, seasoned to taste with oil, lemon juice, salt and pepper, fill the cups fashioned from the whites of the eggs, and arrange them around the tomatoes. Strew chopped shallot and sweet pepper over the endive. Mix equal portions of oil and vinegar, add salt and pepper to taste, and pour over the salad. Serve at once.

## Salmon Salad.

(*For evening company, or fish course at a dinner party.*)

INGREDIENTS.

- Hard-boiled eggs.
- 1 teaspoonful of gelatine, softened in one tablespoonful of cold water.
- 1 pint of string beans or asparagus tips.
- 1 pint of cooked peas.
- French dressing.
- 2 slices of salmon, 2 inches thick.
- Jelly mayonnaise, or fancy butter.
- Capers.

*Method.*—Cut the eggs into halves lengthwise; cut a thin slice from the round ends, that the pieces may be set upright; dip lightly in the gelatine dissolved over hot water, and arrange *miroton* fashion around an oval serving-dish. Set aside, that the eggs may become fixed in position. Marinate the vegetables, separately, with French dressing; cook the salmon by the directions previously given; remove the skin and cover the sides with jelly mayonnaise or fancy butter. When cold decorate with whites of eggs and capers. Use the trimmings from the eggs, and fix them in place by dipping in jelly mayonnaise. Set aside for the decorations to become fixed. Drain the vegetables and arrange inside the border, higher in the centre. Lay the decorated slices of fish upon opposite sides of the mound, and serve either with or without mayonnaise.

## Halibut Salad.

(*For evening company, or fish course at a dinner party.*)

INGREDIENTS.

- A slice of chicken halibut, 3 inches thick.
- 3 cups of cooked peas.
- French dressing.
- Hard-boiled eggs.
- 3 slices of pickled beet.
- 1 teaspoonful of gelatine.
- Jelly mayonnaise, or green butter.
- Heart leaves of lettuce.
- 2 olives.

*Method.*—Prepare the eggs and fasten to the plate as in salmon salad. Dip diamond-shaped pieces of pickled beet in the dissolved gelatine and place upon the front and top of each half of egg. Spread the edge of the fish, after removing the skin, with jelly mayonnaise, or green butter, and, when set, decorate with figures cut from the cooked white of an egg. With forcing-bag and tube shape a pattern around the upper edge of the fish. Place the fish in the centre of the crown or *miroton* of eggs, with the peas seasoned with French dressing around it; cover the place from which the bone was taken with the centre of a head of lettuce, cut in halves, and two fine olives. Serve with a bowl of mayonnaise.

See page 64

## Shells of Fish and Mushrooms.

Cut cold fish—salmon, halibut, lobster, etc.—into small cubes, mix with one-third in measure of cooked mushrooms, also cut small, and add for each cup of mushrooms and fish one tablespoonful of gherkins cut fine. Season with French dressing and let stand one hour; then drain, and mix with jellied mayonnaise. Fill chilled shells with this preparation, rounding it on the top. Make smooth, and mask with jellied mayonnaise. Decorate with gherkins and the white of a hard-boiled egg cut in fanciful shapes, and with stars of mayonnaise.

## Oysters in Aspic Jelly.

Parboil, drain, cool, and wipe dry one quart of oysters. Make a pint of mayonnaise sauce with aspic jelly and coat the well-dried oysters with the sauce. Prepare a quart of chicken aspic. Dip in half-set aspic the white of egg, poached and cut in fanciful shapes, and small gherkins cut in thin slices, and decorate the bottom and sides of a charlotte or cylindrical mould standing in ice water. Pour in jelly to the depth of half an inch; when set, arrange the oysters on it in a circle, one overlapping another; pour in more jelly, and, when set, dispose upon it another circle of oysters. Continue this order until the mould is filled. When removed from the mould, garnish with chopped aspic and fans cut from gherkins and lettuce. Serve with the remainder of the pint of mayonnaise.

## Oyster=and=Celery Salad.

Parboil the oysters (heating them to the boiling-point in their own liquor), drain, and, if large, halve each; marinate with a French dressing (*i.e.*, toss the bits of oyster in oil enough to coat them nicely; then toss them in a little lemon juice, dust with salt and pepper, and set aside to become thoroughly chilled). When ready to serve, drain again and add about one-third as much in bulk of fine-chopped celery and one or two tablespoonfuls of pickled nasturtium seeds or capers; then mix with mayonnaise or a boiled dressing. Serve on a bed of lettuce leaves. Cabbage, sliced as for slaw, may be used in the place of celery. Garnish with small pickles cut in thin slices and spread to resemble a fan.

## Oyster=and=Sweetbread Salad.

Cut a pair of cold cooked sweetbreads into cubes. Parboil one pint of oysters, drain, cool, and cut in halves; marinate the sweetbreads and oysters with French dressing, and allow them to stand at least half an hour; drain, mix with mayonnaise, and serve on a bed of lettuce or cress. Or, surround with a circle of chopped cucumbers seasoned with French dressing.

## Shrimp Salad in Cucumber Boats.

Pare the cucumbers, which should be rather short, and cut them in halves lengthwise; remove the seeds and steam until tender; chill, and arrange on lettuce leaves, or on a bed of watercress. Clean and marinate the shrimps. If large, divide into two or three pieces. Mix with mayonnaise and place in the cucumbers. Decorate with stars of mayonnaise and whole shrimps.

## Shrimp Salad with Aspic Border.

Set a border mould in ice water; dip hard-boiled eggs, cut in halves lengthwise and trimmed to fit the mould, in aspic jelly, and press against the sides of the mould alternately with small vegetable balls, or peas dipped in half-set aspic; fill gradually the empty space in the mould with partly cooled jelly, adding vegetables here and there if desired. Dip in hot water and turn from the mould. Fill in the centre with lettuce, torn in pieces, and one pint of shrimps, broken in pieces and dressed with French dressing. Smooth the mound and mask with jelly mayonnaise. Decorate with shrimps and small heart leaves of lettuce.

**Shell of Fish and Mushrooms.**
See page 65

**Shrimp Salad in Cucumber Boat.**
See page 67

## Shrimp Salad with Aspic Border, No. 2.

Decorate the sides of a ring mould, chilled, with hard-boiled eggs cut in halves, alternated with hearts of lettuce cut in halves; dip the egg and lettuce in half-set aspic, and they will adhere to the sides of the mould. Then proceed as above.

## Shrimp Salad.

Take the shrimps from the shells, reserve the most perfect for garnishing, and break the others into pieces; marinate with French dressing. When ready to serve, drain, and mix with shredded lettuce, or celery cut fine, and mayonnaise. Shape in a mound on a bed of lettuce leaves and mask with mayonnaise. Use capers or olives, chopped very fine, to mark out five or six designs on the mound; a scroll effect is always pretty. Fill in the designs with shrimps and the rest of the mound with capers, sifted yolks or chopped whites of cooked eggs; or fill the designs with the capers or eggs and the rest of the mound with shrimps. Finish with a tuft of lettuce at the top.

## Scallop Salad.

Soak the scallops in salted water (a tablespoonful of salt to a quart of water) one hour; rinse in cold water, cover with boiling water, and let simmer five or six minutes. Rinse again in cold water, drain, and when cold cut into slices. Cut white stalks of celery into small pieces. Mix the celery and scallops—half as much celery as scallops—with mayonnaise or boiled dressing, and shape in a mound. Mask the mound with a thin coating of mayonnaise. With large-sized capers outline a design on each of the four sides of the mound, fill these with whites of eggs, cooked and chopped fine. Ornament with figures cut from slices of boiled beets. Fill in the spaces around the designs with capers, and garnish with green celery leaves and white stalks of celery, fringed.

## Sardine Salad.

Lay the sardines upon soft paper, that they may be freed from oil. Scrape off the skin and remove the bones; squeeze over them a little lemon juice. Arrange upon a bed of crisp lettuce leaves, or upon shredded lettuce, and dress with either French or mayonnaise dressing. Garnish with hard-boiled eggs cut in slices.

## Sardine Salad, No. 2.

Arrange a pint of cold cooked fish, flaked, on a bed of lettuce leaves and cover with sardine dressing. Carefully split six selected sardines; remove the bones and arrange the halves on the top of the salad, with the heads at the centre. Garnish with slices of lemon.

**Shrimp Salad, Border of Eggs in Aspic.**
See page 68

**Lobster Salad.**

**Sardine=and=Egg Salad.**

Skin and bone a dozen sardines and put them in a mortar; remove the shells from an equal number of hard-boiled eggs and cut them into halves crosswise, so as to form cups with pointed edges; put the yolks into the mortar with the sardines, add a tablespoonful, or less, of chopped parsley, a dash of pepper and salt, and work to a smooth paste; moisten with salad dressing and season to taste with salt and pepper. Cut a thin slice from the ends of the egg cups, that they may be set upright on the serving-dish, and fill with the mixture, making it round on the top like a whole yolk. Arrange these on a bed of watercress, or shredded lettuce, and sprinkle plentifully with French dressing.

**Lobster Salad.**

Cut lobster meat in dice and marinate with French dressing. Keep on ice until ready to serve, then drain carefully. Make cups of the inside leaves of lettuce, put a spoonful of the lobster meat in the centre of each cup, and press mayonnaise dressing through a pastry bag with star tube attached on the top of the lobster in each nest. Or, arrange the lobster in a mound on a bed of lettuce leaves, and mask the mound with mayonnaise. Finish the centre with a little bouquet of the heart leaves of lettuce; sift dried coral in a circle about it, and below that arrange circles of sifted yolk or chopped white of egg alternately with the coral. Garnish with the fans and feelers of the lobster. Or, arrange as before, then finish the centre with a bouquet of heart leaves of lettuce and the head of the lobster. Garnish with stars of mayonnaise and fans from the tail.

## Lobster Salad, No. 2.

Remove the flesh carefully from the shell of a lobster, so as to keep the shell of body and tail intact; wash and dry the shell and arrange on a bed of lettuce leaves. Marinate the flesh, cut into cubes, with French dressing. After an hour drain, mix with an equal quantity of shredded lettuce, and replace in the shell. Garnish with mayonnaise and the lobster coral. Dry the coral thoroughly, after which it may be passed readily through a sieve.

## Lobster Salad, No. 3.

### INGREDIENTS.

- 2 good-sized lobsters.
- Lettuce.
- Mayonnaise, or sauce tartare.
- Lobster cutlets.
- 2 tablespoonfuls of butter.
- 1/3 a cup of flour.
- Salt and paprica.
- 1 cup of milk.
- Lobster coral.
- 1 tablespoonful of butter.
- 1 yolk of egg.
- 1 teaspoonful of lemon juice.

- 2 cups of lobster meat.
- 3 cups of aspic jelly.

*Method.*—Make a white sauce of the butter, flour, seasonings and milk; add the coral and butter, after pounding until smooth in a mortar, also the yolk of egg, beaten and diluted with the lemon juice, and the lobster meat chopped rather coarsely. When cold shape into cutlets, dust over with sifted coral, and insert a bit of feeler or claw into the small end of each. Pour a little aspic into a dish, and, when it sets, arrange the cutlets upon it a little distance apart; pour over each a few spoonfuls of aspic, and when set cover with more aspic. When cold and very firm cut out the cutlets, giving a border of aspic to each.

Marinate the flesh of the other lobster, cut into cubes, with French dressing; pile in a mound on a bed of lettuce leaves. Insert a tuft of leaves in the top, and arrange the cutlets against the mound. Garnish with feelers and claws. Serve mayonnaise or sauce tartare with the salad.

**Bluefish Salad.**
See page 75

**Litchi Nut and Orange Salad.**
See page 88

## Lobster Salad in Ring of Aspic.

Set a ring mould in ice water. In the bottom of the mould arrange pitted olives or pim-olas an inch apart. Dip figures, cut from slices of royal custard, or from cooked carrot or turnip, into liquid aspic, and place them on the sides of the mould, to which they will adhere; dip large-sized capers (a larding-needle or skewer is of assistance in this work) in aspic and with them ornament the mould; then fill with aspic and set aside to become fixed. When ready to serve, dip the mould in hot water and invert on a serving-dish. Cut the meat from two two-pound lobsters into small cubes. Season with French dressing. Fill the open space in the aspic with the salad; garnish the top with the feelers and delicate lettuce leaves, and arrange a wreath of lettuce leaves around the aspic. Stamp out rounds of bread; stamp again with the same cutter to form crescents, spread delicately with butter, and then with caviare seasoned with a few drops of lemon juice, and dispose symmetrically on the lettuce.

## Mousseline of Lobster as a Salad.

Chill timbale moulds in ice water; dip thin slices of gherkins into half-set aspic, and arrange them symmetrically against the sides of the moulds, and brush over the decoration with aspic. Cut the claw meat of a two-pound lobster into small cubes; chop fine, and pound the remaining meat in a mortar; then add to it the liver and fat, and pass through a sieve. There should be about one cup. Simmer the shell in water to cover half an hour. Beat the yolks of three eggs, slightly, with one-fourth a teaspoonful of salt and a dash of paprica; add one cup of the lobster liquor very gradually, and cook over hot water as a boiled custard. Remove from the fire and add one-fourth a package of gelatine, softened in one-fourth a cup of cold lobster liquor, or chicken stock; strain over the sifted lobster meat and stir occasionally over ice water; when it begins to set, add the lobster dice, and fold in carefully one cup of whipped cream. Turn the mixture into the decorated mould, and, when set, turn out on to lettuce leaves. Decorate with the head, feelers and claws of the lobster. Serve with French or mayonnaise dressing. French dressing is preferable with so rich a mixture.

**Moulded Salmon Salad.**
See page 75

**Salad of Shrimps and Bamboo Sprouts.**

## Anchovy Salad.

INGREDIENTS.

- 8 salted anchovies, or 12 bottled anchovies.
- 4 hard-boiled eggs.
- 1 head of lettuce.
- Juice of half a small lemon.
- French or mayonnaise dressing, or Sauce tartare.

*Method.*—If salt anchovies are to be used, soak them in cold water two hours, then drain, dry, and remove skin and bones; divide the flesh into small pieces and squeeze the lemon juice over them. When ready to serve, arrange the lettuce leaves upon a serving-dish, stalk ends at the centre, cut the eggs in slices, mix with the bits of anchovies, and arrange upon the lettuce. Pour a French or mayonnaise dressing made with onion juice, or a sauce tartare, over the salad.

## Salad of Lettuce, Bamboo Sprouts, and Shrimps.

Marinate a cup of shrimps, broken in small pieces, with three tablespoonfuls of oil, one tablespoonful of lemon juice, a dash of salt and pepper. Select the tender bamboo sprouts in a can, and cut them into small pieces of the shape desired. When ready to serve, dress these with salt, pepper, oil, and lemon juice. Use three measures of oil to one of acid. Begin with the oil. Continue mixing and adding oil, until each piece is glossy. Then add the acid. Mix the prepared sprouts and the drained shrimps, and turn them onto a bed of lettuce, cut in narrow shreds, and dressed with oil and acid. Decorate the salad with heart leaves of lettuce, whole shrimps, and hollow sections of bamboo, cut in thin slices.

## Bluefish Salad (excellent).

Separate the remnants of a baked bluefish into flakes, discarding skin and bones. Set aside, covered, until cold. About an hour before serving, sprinkle with salt and pepper and (for a generous pint of fish) the juice of a lemon. When ready to serve, dispose heart leaves of lettuce on the edge of a salad plate, and turn the fish into the centre, letting it come out over the stems of the lettuce leaves. Pour a boiled dressing over the top, and spread evenly (with a silver knife) over the fish. Put a tablespoonful of chopped pickled beet at the stems of each group of leaves, a ring of the beet near the top, and figures, cut from the beet, between.

## Moulded Salmon Salad.

Use a pound of salmon, fresh-cooked or canned. Remove skin and bone, and pick the flesh fine with a silver fork. Mix half a teaspoonful of salt, a teaspoonful of sugar, a teaspoonful of flour, half a teaspoonful of mustard, and a dash of paprica. Over these pour very gradually three-fourths a cup of hot milk and stir and cook over hot water ten minutes, then add one-fourth a cup of hot vinegar and two tablespoonfuls of butter creamed and mixed with the beaten yolks of two eggs; stir until the egg is set, then add one level tablespoonful of granulated gelatine, softened in one-fourth a cup of cold water, and strain over the salmon; mix thoroughly, and turn into a mould. When chilled serve with Cream Salad Dressing (page 27), to which half a cucumber, chopped fine and drained, has been added. Reserve a part of the dressing, omitting the cucumber, and use with slices of cucumber as a garnish. To prepare the cucumber, pare with a handy slicer and cut from it a section three-fourths an inch thick; pare this round and round very thin and roll loosely to form a cup. Dispose this on the top of the fish and fill with dressing. (Use a pastry bag and tube.) Cut the rest of the cucumber in thin slices.

# VARIOUS COMPOUND SALADS.

Give us the luxuries of life, and we will dispense with its necessaries.—*Motley.*

Three several salads have I sacrificed, bedew'd with precious oil and vinegar.—*Beaumont and Fletcher.*

### Sweetbread=and=Cucumber Salad.

Arrange the leaves of a head of cabbage lettuce loosely upon a serving-dish, without destroying its shape. Have ready a pair of sweetbreads cooked in salted, acidulated water twenty minutes, and cooled and cut in small cubes and marinated; also the same quantity of cucumber cut in dice, chilled in ice water and dried upon a cloth. Drain the French dressing from the sweetbread and scatter the bits of sweetbread and cucumber through the lettuce. Press three-fourths a cup of firm jelly mayonnaise through a pastry bag with small tube, in little stars, here and there, throughout the lettuce, and serve at once.

### Sweetbread=and=Cucumber Salad, No. 2.

Cook, marinate and drain the sweetbreads as before; mix with an equal quantity of cucumber cut in dice, and then with cream dressing. Line the inner side of lettuce nests with slices of radish, one overlapping another (do not remove the pink skin from the radish). Put in a spoonful of the salad and garnish each nest with a small radish cut to resemble a flower.

## Chicken Salad.

Use two parts of cold cooked chicken to one part of celery. Marinate and drain the chicken, add the celery, and mix with mayonnaise or boiled dressing. Arrange the salad in nests of lettuce leaves and put a pim-ola in the centre of each nest.

## Chicken Salad, No. 2.

Prepare the salad as before; dispose in a mound on a bed of lettuce leaves and mask with mayonnaise. By the use of stoned olives, cut in halves, divide the surface into quarters. Fill two opposite sections with whites of eggs chopped fine, a third with capers or olives chopped fine, and the fourth with sifted yolks of eggs. Garnish with lettuce and curled celery.

## French Chicken Salad.

Cook the meats of English walnuts in well-seasoned chicken stock until tender; remove the brown skin and break in pieces; when cold mix with chicken and celery, and proceed as in preceding recipes. The walnuts give the salad a flavor similar to that produced in France by the use of truffles.

## Chicken=and=Fresh=Mushroom Salad.

Peel mushroom caps, break in pieces, and sauté in melted butter five or six minutes with a slice of onion; add chicken liquor or hot water and let simmer until tender. Remove from the liquor, cover, and set aside to cool.

Add the liquor and the peelings and stalks of the mushrooms to the liquid in which the chicken is to be cooked. Use the chicken and mushrooms with celery or lettuce in any recipe for chicken salad.

### Chicken Salad, No. 3.

Arrange the salad upon the centre of the dish and mask with mayonnaise; then with pastry bag and tube pipe the dressing in some fanciful design. Surround with a border of aspic jelly, tinted a delicate green. The jelly may be cut in blocks or triangles, or into small cubes, and then massed about the salad. Cut the aspic in a cold room; first dip the knife in hot water and wipe dry.

### Chicken Salad, No. 4.

Cut one cucumber and one bunch of round radishes in thin slices, and add two-thirds a cup of shredded celery. Season with four tablespoonfuls of oil, two tablespoonfuls of vinegar or lemon juice, half a teaspoonful of salt and a dash of paprica. Put on a bed of shredded lettuce or on heart leaves of lettuce; cover with three cups of chicken cut in cubes and marinated an hour or more with four tablespoonfuls of oil, two tablespoonfuls of lemon juice or vinegar, half a teaspoonful of salt and a dash of white pepper. Mask with mayonnaise. Arrange some bits of celery, an inch and a half in length and curled on one end, about the salad, with a bit of yolk of egg in the centre of each. Or, instead of the celery and yolk of egg, use sliced radishes (do not remove the red skin), having the slices overlap one another. Finish the top with tuft of lettuce or curled celery and yolk of egg.

### Mushroom Salad with Medallions of Chicken.

Bone a chicken, fill with forcemeat, and cook until tender in stock; then press between two dishes until cold. Cut in slices and stamp in rounds. Stamp out an equal number of rounds from cooked tongue. Spread these with "green butter" (see [Green-Butter Sandwiches](Green-Butter Sandwiches)) and place the rounds of chicken evenly on the tops. Coat these with white chaud-froid sauce and decorate in some design with truffles, ham or tongue. When the sauce has set, brush over the medallions with aspic jelly, cold but not set. When thoroughly cold stamp out with a round cutter. Drain and dry a can of white button mushrooms; toss them about in cold aspic until they are well coated. When the jelly has become fixed about them, pile high in the centre of a serving-dish; arrange the medallions about them, resting on delicate leaves of lettuce. Serve mayonnaise or tartare sauce with the salad. Sweetbreads may be substituted for the chicken, and fresh mushrooms for the canned.

## Mousse=de=Poulet Salad.

Scald one cup of milk, cream or *well-reduced* chicken stock (the last is preferable); beat the yolks of three eggs slightly, add one-fourth a teaspoonful, each, of common salt and celery salt, and a dash of paprica, and cook as a boiled custard. Remove from the fire and add one-fourth a package of gelatine (one tablespoonful of granulated gelatine), softened in one-fourth a cup of chicken liquor or water. Strain over half a cup of cooked chicken (white meat), chopped and pounded in a mortar and passed through a sieve. Stir over ice water until the mixture is perfectly smooth and begins to set, then fold into it one cup of whipped cream. Turn into a ring mould, and, when chilled and well set, turn on to a bed of lettuce and fill in the centre with equal parts of celery and English walnuts, blanched, sliced and mixed with a French dressing.

The half-cup of chicken, well pressed down, should weigh four ounces. The chicken broth should be strong and well flavored. Either one cup of whipped cream, or one cup of cream, whipped, may be used. The latter gives a firmer mousse, more pronounced in flavor; the former, a mousse of a lighter and more delicate consistency, and one more delicate in flavor.

### Mousse=de=Poulet, No. 2.

Mould the mousse in small cups; turn out on to a slice of chilled tomato resting upon a lettuce leaf; garnish with mayonnaise dressing, decorating both the tomato and the mousse.

### Mousse=de=Poulet, No. 3.

Mould the mousse in a ring mould and fill in the centre with equal parts of cucumber or asparagus tips and diced sweetbread; marinate the sweetbread with French dressing, and drain thoroughly before mixing with the cucumber or asparagus. Garnish with mayonnaise dressing.

### Mousse=de=Poulet, No. 4.

Fill in the centre of the ring with diced cucumbers and sliced radishes, mixed with cream dressing. Garnish with cream dressing, using pastry bag and tube, and radishes cut to resemble roses.

### Mousse=de=Poulet, No. 5.

Fill in the centre of the ring with mushrooms and sweetbread dressed with a French dressing. If the button mushrooms (canned) are used, cut in quarters; if fresh mushrooms are at hand, remove the stems and peel the caps; break into pieces and sauté in a little hot butter; then add hot water or stock and let simmer until tender (fifteen or twenty minutes). Drain and chill before using.

## Turkey=and=Chestnut Salad.

Prepare the chestnuts as previously directed, using twice as much turkey meat, light or dark, cut into small cubes. Serve with lettuce and French, boiled or mayonnaise dressing, as desired. Marinate and drain the meat before adding the nuts.

## Duck=and=Olive Salad.

Cut the meat from a duck in small pieces, and slice pim-olas very thin; use two tablespoonfuls of pim-olas to a cup of meat. Serve on a bed of cress with a French dressing.

## Duck=and=Orange Salad.

Slice the oranges lengthwise; use twice as much flesh as fruit. Dress with oil, salt and paprica, and serve on lettuce leaves.

## Ham Salad.

Soak half a tablespoonful of granulated gelatine in one tablespoonful and a half of cold water, and dissolve in three-fourths a cup of hot chicken liquor. Strain over one cup of chopped ham and stir until the mixture begins to thicken, then fold in one cup of *thick* cream beaten stiff; add, also, a few grains of paprica and salt, if needed. Mould in a ring mould, and, when set and cold, turn from the mould; fill in the centre with lettuce arranged like a cup, and fill the cup with mayonnaise. Or, serve with French dressing.

**Spinach and Egg Salad.**
See page 86

**Marguerite Salad.**
See page 86

## Bacon Salad.

Cut six or eight slices of tender bacon into small squares and fry until they are delicately browned; then drain on soft paper. Heat six tablespoonfuls of the fat and two tablespoonfuls of vinegar or lemon juice; beat together the yolks of three eggs and one-fourth a teaspoonful, each, of paprica and mustard, and cook with the fat and vinegar over hot water until the mixture thickens slightly. When the dressing is cold cut a head of lettuce into narrow ribbons, toss the lettuce and bits of bacon together, and mix with the dressing. Serve at once.

## Italian Salad.

(Miss Cohen.)

Ingredients.

- 2 herrings, soaked in milk over night.
- 3 boiled potatoes, cut in very small dice.
- 2 tablespoonfuls of cucumber pickles, chopped fine.
- 1 tablespoonful of capers, chopped fine.
- 2 small boiled beets, cut fine.
- ½ a pound (1 cup) of cold roast chicken, cut fine.
- ½ a pound (1 cup) of boiled tongue, cut fine.
- 2 apples, pared and finely chopped.
- 2 carrots, cooked and finely chopped.
- 1 celery root, cooked and chopped.
- ½ a cup of pecan nuts, broken fine.
- A little onion juice.

*Method.*—Mix the ingredients together thoroughly; add mayonnaise to moisten well. Serve on a flat dish. Mask the top with mayonnaise, then divide into squares like a checker-board, using fine-shredded pimento or pickled beet to mark the divisions; fill in alternate squares with sifted yolk of hard-boiled egg and the remaining squares with chopped white of egg. Garnish the edge with parsley, and set in the centre half a hard-boiled egg cut lengthwise in points and filled with capers.

## Pâté de Foie Gras, Moulded in Aspic.

Cover the bottoms of small-sized timbale moulds with a little aspic jelly; decorate the jelly with bits of royal custard and capers; cover with more aspic; then add, alternately, layers of *pâté de foie gras* and aspic, until the mould is filled. Turn on to shredded lettuce and garnish with mayonnaise, using pastry bag and tube. Arrange on individual dishes, so as not to disarrange the dressing in serving. Or, garnish with a chopped cucumber dressed with French dressing.

# Spinach=and=Tongue Salad.

INGREDIENTS.

- ¼ a peck of spinach.
- 1 tablespoonful of lemon juice.
- ¼ a teaspoonful of salt.
- A dash of paprica.
- 1 tablespoonful of oil or butter.
- Slices of cold tongue.
- Sauce tartare.

*Method.*—Cook the spinach in salted boiling water until tender; drain, and chop very fine, and season with salt, pepper, oil and lemon juice. Press into small, well-buttered moulds or cups. Have ready thin, round slices of cold boiled or braised tongue, the slices a trifle larger than the cups of spinach. When the spinach is cold turn it from the moulds on to the rounds of tongue, and press a star of sauce tartare on the top of each mould. Garnish with parsley and slices of lemon.

**Easter Salad.**

**Country Salad.**

See page 87

## Spinach=and=Egg Salad.

(See cut facing page 84.)

Prepare and mould the spinach as in the preceding recipe. Have ready, also, some cold boiled eggs and mayonnaise. Turn the spinach from the moulds on to nests of shredded lettuce. Dispose, chain fashion, around the base of the spinach, the whites of the eggs cut in rings, and press a star of mayonnaise in the centre of each ring. Pass the yolks through a sieve and sprinkle over the tops of the mounds, and place above this the round ends of the whites.

## Marguerite Salad.

(See cut facing page 84.)

Arrange garden cress on a serving-dish; in the centre dispose whites of hard-boiled eggs cut in eighths lengthwise, to resemble the petals of a flower, and sift the yolks into the centre. When ready to serve, sprinkle with French dressing and toss together.

## Easter Salad.

With the smooth sides of butter-hands roll Neufchatel cheese into small egg shapes. Cut long radishes into straws and season with French dressing. Scatter the straws in lettuce nests, arrange the eggs in the nests, sprinkle with dressing, and fleck with chopped parsley or paprica.

## Easter Salad, No. 2.

Arrange flat nests of shredded lettuce on individual plates. Cut a five-cent Neufchatel cheese in three pieces; roll each piece into a ball and flatten to resemble the white of a poached egg, having the cheese about one-fourth an inch in thickness. These may be shaped upon a plate and then removed carefully with a spatula to the nests of lettuce. With pastry bag and plain tube put a mound of mayonnaise on the centre of each cake of cheese, to represent the yolk of an egg. Serve thoroughly chilled. A dash of pepper (paprica preferred) may decorate the top of the dressing.

## Country Salad.

(See cut facing page 86.)

Cut cold boiled corned beef or tongue into thin strips and pile in the centre of a serving-dish. Cook potato balls in meat broth until tender; blanch and cool, roll in mayonnaise or boiled dressing, and dispose about the meat. About these put a ring of celery cut fine, then cooked carrot and turnip cut in straws. Garnish with parsley and cucumber pickles cut in fans. Serve with additional dressing.

## Orange=and=Litchi Nut Salad.

Peel the oranges and cut them into lengthwise slices. Crush the shells of the nuts, take out the meats, and remove the stones; cut the nut meats in halves. Mix the nuts with oil, a tablespoonful to a cup, and sprinkle the orange slices with oil; add also a little lemon juice if the oranges are sweet. Garnish with slices of orange from which the skin has not been taken, also, if desired, with lettuce dressed with French dressing. The oil and lettuce may be omitted, using sugar in place; little, however, will be needed, as the nuts are sweet, tasting much like raisins.

## Green=and=White Salad.

Cut cooked chicken or sweetbreads in half-inch cubes; remove the skin and seeds from white grapes, and cut each grape in halves; cut tender blanched celery stalks in small pieces. Take equal portions of celery and meat and half as much of seeded grapes. Mix with French dressing; the meat should stand in the dressing an hour or more, when ready to serve. Serve in nests of lettuce. Dispose a little white mayonnaise or cream dressing on each nest. Garnish with halves of blanched pistachio nuts.

# FRUIT AND NUT SALADS.

"Fat olives and pistachio's fragrant nut,
And the pine's tasteful apple."

### Fruit Salad.

(*Sweet, to serve with cake.*)

Peel and slice four bananas, also four oranges, lengthwise, carefully removing pith and seeds. Dissect half a ripe pineapple, taking the pulp from the core in small pieces with a silver fork. Hull and wash a part of a basket of strawberries. Arrange the fruit in the salad-bowl, making each layer smaller than the preceding. Pour over the dressing given below, and serve thoroughly chilled.

### Dressing for Fruit Salad.

(*Sweet.*)

Boil one cup of sugar and half a cup of water five minutes, then pour on to the beaten yolks of three eggs; return to the fire and cook over hot water, stirring constantly until thickened slightly; cool, and add the juice of two lemons. Half a cup of wine may be used in the place of the lemon juice, retaining one tablespoonful of the lemon juice.

### Fruit Salad.

(*June.*)

Pare lengthwise a *ripe* pineapple and remove the eyes. With a fork dislodge from the hard centre the single fruits (the lines left by the bracts will indicate the places where the divisions should be made). Slice *lengthwise* three sweet oranges, after removing the peel and white skin. Peel and slice two bananas, and cut in halves lengthwise one cup of strawberries. If the fruit be sweet, use the juice of half a lemon, otherwise omit it. Beat to an emulsion one-fourth a cup of olive oil, one tablespoonful of honey, and, if needed, the lemon juice; toss the fruit, together or separately, in the dressing, and serve on delicate leaves of lettuce. The most striking effect is produced by dressing each kind of fruit separately, thus massing each color by itself. When new figs are seasonable, they may be used in fruit salads to take the place of the honey. If the pineapple be of large size, more dressing will be required.

## Fruit=and=Nut Salad.

Peel neatly three oranges and slice them lengthwise; also cut three bananas in thin slices. Skin and seed half a pound of white grapes, and blanch and slice the meats of one-fourth a pound of English walnuts. Serve very cold on lettuce leaves, dressed with four tablespoonfuls of oil, two tablespoonfuls of lemon juice—less, if the oranges are sour—and half a teaspoonful of salt.

## Fruit=and=Nut Salad, No. 2.

Skin and seed half a pound of white grapes; blanch and slice half a pound of English walnuts or almonds. Toss with four tablespoonfuls of oil, one-fourth a teaspoonful of salt and two tablespoonfuls of lemon juice. Serve in nests of lettuce. Garnish the nests with maraschino cherries.

## Cherry Salad.

(Mrs. Peterson.)

Marinate as many hazelnuts as cherries with plenty of oil, half as much lemon juice as oil, and a little salt, one or two hours. Put a nut in the place of the stone in the cherries. Sprinkle with oil and a very little lemon juice, and serve in lettuce nests.

## Fruit Salad.

(*Winter.*)

Peel two oranges; with a sharp knife cut between the pulp and the skin and remove the section entire. Slice the meats of one-fourth a pound of English walnuts. Of one-fourth a pound of figs select a few for a garnish and cut the rest in thin slices. Slice three bananas. Toss half the ingredients with two or three tablespoonfuls of oil, and, if the oranges are sweet, toss again with one tablespoonful of lemon juice. Arrange in a mound on a salad-dish. Put the rest of the fruit, each kind separately, on the mound in sections; garnish the edge and top with heart leaves of lettuce, and add stars of mayonnaise and candied cherries here and there.

## Orange=and=Walnut Salad.

This is a particularly good salad to serve with game. Select fine oranges, remove the peel and every particle of white skin, and slice very thin lengthwise. Slice English walnuts, blanched or plain. To each pint of orange slices add half a pint (scant) of the sliced nuts; dress with three tablespoonfuls of oil, one-fourth a teaspoonful of salt, and, if the oranges are particularly sweet, a tablespoonful of lemon juice. Serve on a bed of watercress or lettuce.

### Celery=and=Chestnut Salad.

Shell and blanch the chestnuts; then boil about fifteen minutes, or until tender; drain and cool. When cool cut into quarters, add an equal quantity of fine-sliced celery, dress with French dressing, and serve on lettuce leaves. Sliced pimentos may be added.

### Apple,=Celery=and=English=Walnut Salad.

Peel and cut the apples in small cubes; blanch the nuts and break in pieces, and cut the celery in thin slices; marinate the apple and nuts with oil and lemon juice half an hour; drain, add the celery and mayonnaise dressing, and serve in cups made by removing the pulp from red apples. Cut the edges of the apples in small vandykes; keep fresh in cold water until ready to serve.

### Orange=and=Banana Salad.

(*Sweet.*)

Stir the juice of two oranges, half a cup of sherry wine, one tablespoonful of lemon juice, half a cup of sugar and the unbeaten white of an egg, over the fire, until the boiling-point is reached; let simmer slowly ten minutes, strain through a cheese-cloth, and, when thoroughly chilled, pour over three bananas and three oranges, sliced and mixed together in a salad-bowl. Sprinkle with half a cup of dessicated cocoanut. Serve thoroughly chilled.

### Fig=and=Nut Salad.

Slice pulled figs, cooked and cooled, and mix with them a few slices of walnuts or blanched almonds. Serve with French dressing made of claret and lemon juice instead of vinegar, or with a cream dressing. In using the cream dressing, mix the ingredients with a little of the dressing and dispose additional dressing here and there, using the forcing-bag and tube. When available, fresh figs are preferable to those that have been cooked.

### Grapefruit Salad.

Cut the chilled fruit in halves, crosswise, and take out the pulp with a spoon; dress with French dressing. The juice of the grapefruit may be used in the place of other acid, and mayonnaise in the place of French dressing. Serve on lettuce leaves, or return to the skin from which the pulp was removed. The edge of the grapefruit cup may be cut in vandykes, or otherwise ornamented.

**Fruit Salad.**
See page 90

**Turquoise Salad, No. 2.**
See page 94

## Turquoise Salad.

Mix together equal parts of celery and tart apple cut in match-like pieces, and one or two pimentos cut in similar pieces. Dress with mayonnaise made light with whipped cream. Serve in nests of lettuce.

## Turquoise Salad, No. 2.

Use pineapple in the place of the apple; serve in a mound on a bed of lettuce leaves. Garnish with stars cut from the pimentos with French cutter, curled celery, and heart leaves of celery.

## Salad Chiffonade.

Seed two green peppers, boil two or three minutes, then cut in shreds. Shred the light and dark leaves of a head of lettuce, or endive, separately. Cut three tomatoes in shreds. Remove the peel and skin from one large grapefruit. Serve with French dressing, seasoning, and then arranging each article separately upon the serving-dish, having a circle of light and then dark green material about the edge.

### Peach=and=Almond Salad.

Blanch the almonds and cut in thin slices. Chill the peaches, peel, and cut in slices; use one-fifth as much in bulk of sliced nuts as sliced peaches. Serve with French dressing, or with mayonnaise made white with whipped cream. Garnish the edge with delicate lettuce leaves and serve at once.

### Peach Salad.

(*English style.*)

Cut ripe, fine-flavored peaches into quarters, after removing the skins. Cover with champagne, thoroughly chilled, and sprinkle with tea-rose petals. Serve at once.

### Peach,=Strawberry=and=Cherry Salad.

(*London style.*)

Let a large handful of fresh rose petals stand an hour or two in a cool place in a cup of Hungarian wine. Strain out the leaves and pour the wine over a quart of mixed fruit,—peaches pared and cut in quarters, strawberries hulled and cut in halves, and cherries stoned,—all thoroughly chilled. Let a handful of rose petals stand an hour or two in a cup of thick cream; then strain the cream, sweeten slightly with powdered sugar, whip to a stiff froth, and use as a garnish for the fruit.

## Grapefruit, Pineapple, and Pimento Salad.

Cut a large grapefruit in halves and remove the pulp with a sharp knife to avoid crushing it; remove half the pulp of a large pineapple from the core with a fork, after carefully removing the unedible outside. Dress with white mayonnaise and serve upon crisp lettuce hearts. Garnish with tiny bits of pimento. 2d.—Omit the pimento, lettuce and mayonnaise, and dress with sherry wine and sugar. For a Christmas salad, use the first formula and canned pineapple if the fresh be not at hand. Dispose the dressed pineapple and grapefruit upon shredded lettuce, having a circle of heart leaves around the edge. Dot here and there with small stars cut from the red pimento with a French cutter. Or chop the pimento fine and dispose in the shape of a large five-pointed star in the centre of the dish.

# HOW TO PREPARE AND USE ASPIC JELLY.

To make aspic for moulding or decorating a fish salad, use stock prepared from chicken or veal, or from fish. For chicken, veal or sweetbread salad, use chicken or veal stock, or a light-colored consommé. In an emergency, aspic may be made from the prepared extracts of beef, or from bouillon capsules. Aspic is often tinted delicately to harmonize with a particular color scheme. A light-green aspic has been found quite effective.

## RECIPE.

To one quart of highly seasoned stock, freed from all fat, add the juice of a lemon, a bay leaf, half a cup of wine and one box of gelatine soaked in a cup of cold water. Beat into the mixture the slightly beaten whites and crushed shells of two eggs. Heat to the boiling-point, stirring constantly, and let boil five minutes. After standing ten minutes skim off the froth, etc., and strain through a cheese-cloth folded double and held in a colander.

### Aspic for Garnishing.

Pour the liquid jelly into a new tin to the depth of half an inch. Wring a napkin out of cold water and spread it smoothly over the meat-board. Dip the pan in warm water and turn the jelly onto the napkin; stamp in rounds, diamonds or other fanciful shapes. If blocks of greater thickness be required, fill the pan to the required depth with the liquid aspic. When turned from the mould, cut in squares or diamonds with a knife, wiped dry after having been dipped in hot water.

## To Chop Jelly.

Cut the jelly slowly, first in one direction, then in the opposite direction. Each piece, whether large or small, should be clean-cut and distinct. Aspic melts or softens in a warm place, and should not be taken from the mould until the time of serving, and then it must be handled with care.

## Consommé for Aspic Jelly.

Cut two pounds of beef from the under part of the round and two pounds of shin of veal into small pieces; crack the bones in the shin. Place over the fire with two and a half quarts of cold water; add one ounce of lean ham. Heat slowly, and cook just below the boiling-point two or three hours; then add to the kettle a three-pound fowl, and allow it to remain till tender. Put some marrow into the frying-pan, and when hot sauté in it a small onion cut fine, two tablespoonfuls, each, of chopped celery, carrot and turnip; add to the soup kettle, removing the fowl, together with a sprig, each, of parsley, thyme and summer savory, two bay leaves, a small blade of mace, four cloves, two peppercorns and one scant tablespoonful of salt. Let simmer about an hour and a half; then strain and let cool.

## Chicken Stock for Aspic Jelly.

Put a four-pound fowl and a few bits of veal from the neck over the fire in three pints of cold water. Heat slowly to the boiling-point, let boil five minutes, then skim and let simmer until the fowl is nearly tender. Now add an onion and half a sliced carrot, a stalk of celery, a teaspoonful of sweet herbs tied in a bag with a sprig of parsley, two cloves, a blade of mace, eight peppercorns and a teaspoonful of salt. Remove the fowl when tender, and let the stock simmer until reduced to about one quart; strain, and set aside to become cool.

## Second Stock for Use in Sauces, Etc.

Break the bones from roasts; add the tough or browned bits of meat and fat; add also the flank ends from chops and steaks, cut small (there should always be a few bits of fresh meat), and cover with cold water. Heat slowly and let simmer two or three hours, then add, for each two quarts of water used, one-fourth a cup, each, of chopped onion and carrot, two stalks of celery and a tomato cut small, two teaspoonfuls of sweet herbs, two sprigs of parsley browned in two tablespoonfuls of butter or drippings, and cook about an hour. Strain and let cool. Stock will keep a day or two in summer and nearly a week in winter, if the cake of fat that forms upon the top be left undisturbed.

## Fish Stock.

*(For use in fish aspic, or any fish dish.)*

Cover the bones and trimmings from the fish that is to be used for the salad with cold water; add, if convenient, the body bones of a lobster or two. Add also one or two pounds of an inexpensive fish, and a pint of water for each pound of fish. All must be fresh. Bring the water slowly to the boiling-point and let simmer an hour, then add, for each quart of water, one tablespoonful, each, of chopped onion and carrot, a sprig of parsley and one teaspoonful of sweet herbs, sautéd delicately in two tablespoonfuls of butter. Season to taste with salt and cayenne.

## Aspic Jelly from Bouillon Capsules, Etc.

Put over the fire one-fourth a cup, each, of onion and carrot, sautéd in two tablespoonfuls of butter, two stalks of celery, a bay leaf, half a dozen peppercorns and two or three cloves, with one quart of water; add three bouillon capsules, or three teaspoonfuls of beef extract (not home-made) dissolved in two cups of boiling water; let simmer about half an hour, then add one box of gelatine softened in one cup of cold water, any additional flavoring desired, and the slightly beaten white and crushed shell of one egg (more shells will be advantageous). Bring slowly to the boiling-point, stirring constantly meanwhile, and let simmer five minutes; let stand in a hot place ten minutes, then skim and strain through a cheese-cloth folded double.

## White Chaud=froid Sauce.

*(For coating joints of fowl or game, or medallions of fowl, tongue or sweetbreads.)*

To one pint of white sauce, made of white stock, add three-fourths a cup of aspic jelly and one tablespoonful of lemon juice; let simmer until reduced to the consistency of very thick cream; remove the butter from the top and let cool slightly before using.

# CHEESE DISHES SERVED WITH SALADS.

### Cheese Custard.

(Mrs. Dimon.)

Butter a baking-dish, put in a layer of bread cut in pieces one inch square with crust removed, sprinkle thin-sliced cheese over the bread, dust with salt and paprica, or a few grains of cayenne. Add other layers of bread and cheese, seasoning as before, using in all half a small loaf of bread, one cup of cheese and half a teaspoonful of salt. Beat two eggs slightly, add one pint of milk, and pour the mixture over the bread and cheese. Bake about half an hour in a moderate oven.

### Cheese Soufflé.

Cook together four tablespoonfuls of butter and two tablespoonfuls of flour, into which have been sifted one-fourth a teaspoonful, each, of soda and mustard and a few grains of cayenne. Add gradually half a cup of milk. When the sauce boils, remove from the fire and stir into it one cup of grated cheese (half a pound) and the yolks of three eggs, beaten until light. When well mixed, fold in the stiffly beaten whites of three eggs. Bake in a buttered pudding-dish, in a moderate oven, about twenty-five minutes, or in individual dishes, paper cases, or china shirring-cups, about twelve minutes. *Serve at once* from the dish or dishes. The soufflé will "stand up" a little better, if three-fourths a cup of milk be used in place of the half-cup as given, and half a cup of stale grated bread be added before the cheese; but it will not be quite so delicate.

**Cheese Ramequins.**

**Individual Soufflé of Cheese.**
See page 108

## Cheese Ramequins.

Put four tablespoonfuls of butter and half a cup of water into a saucepan. When these boil, add half a cup of flour and a few grains, each, of salt and paprica; cook and stir until the mixture cleaves from the pan. Turn into a mixing-bowl and beat in two ounces of grated Parmesan cheese; then beat in, one at a time, two eggs. On a well-buttered baking-sheet shape the paste into flat circular pieces about an inch in diameter. Brush over the tops with beaten egg, diluted with one or two tablespoonfuls of milk or water, and put three or four dice of cheese on each. Bake about fifteen minutes. Serve very hot.

## Cheese Straws.

Roll plain or puff paste into a rectangular sheet one-fourth an inch thick. Sprinkle one-half with grated cheese (any kind of cheese will do, but Parmesan is preferred); also add a few grains of cayenne and salt. Fold the other half over this and press the edges together closely. Fold again to make three layers, turn half-way round, pat and roll out to the thickness of one-fourth an inch. Sprinkle one half with cheese and proceed as before. Continue rolling and adding the cheese, until, to one cup and a half of flour, from half to a whole cup of cheese has been used. After the last rolling, cut into bands half an inch wide, or into rings and straws one-fourth an inch wide. The straws and bands should be four or five inches in length, and the rings large enough to hold three or four straws. Serve the bands piled in log-cabin style on a doylie-covered plate. If the paste be made expressly for the straws, the cheese and cayenne may be mixed into the flour with the butter, thus diminishing time in making. Bake in a moderate oven until delicately browned.

### Gnochi à la Romaine.

Melt four tablespoonfuls of butter; cook in it four tablespoonfuls, each, of cornstarch and flour and half a teaspoonful of salt, then add gradually one pint of milk. When thick and smooth stir in the beaten yolks of two eggs, add four tablespoonfuls of grated Parmesan cheese, and spread on a buttered pan to cool. Just before serving, cut the paste in shapes, lay on a baking-sheet, and brown delicately in the oven.

### Cheese Balls.

Mix together thoroughly one cup and a half of grated cheese, one tablespoonful of flour, one-fourth, a teaspoonful of salt and a few grains of cayenne; then add the whites of three eggs, beaten stiff. Shape in small balls and roll in cracker crumbs, sifted or crushed to a fine meal; fry in deep fat and drain on soft paper.

## Individual Soufflés of Cheese, Iced.

(See cut facing page 106.)

Mix half a cup of grated Parmesan and one-fourth a cup of grated Gruyère cheese and one-fourth a teaspoonful of paprika with two-thirds a cup of chicken aspic, cold, but not set. Stir over ice water until just beginning to form, then fold into it one cup of whipped cream. Fasten strips of white paper around paper soufflé cases, letting the strips rise an inch and a half above the cases, fixing in place with sealing-wax, mucilage, or a stitch. Fill the cases and the papers surrounding them with the cheese mixture, and set them in a pail or mould that is thoroughly chilled. Press the cover down over a paper, and pack in equal parts of ice and salt. Let stand an hour. Before serving, remove the paper, sprinkle the tops with buttered crumbs, browned, and serve at once.

## Cheese Croquettes.

(Touraine.)

Ingredients.

- 3 tablespoonfuls of butter.
- ¼ a cup of flour.
- 2/3 a cup of milk.
- Yolks of 2 eggs.
- 1 cup of mild cheese, cut in small cubes.
- ½ a cup of grated Gruyère cheese.
- Salt and cayenne to taste.

*Method.*—Make a sauce of the butter, flour and milk; add the yolks, slightly beaten, and beat thoroughly; add the grated cheese, and, when melted, remove from the fire; add the seasonings and cubes of cheese.

Spread in a shallow pan to cool. Cut in any shape desired, dip in crumbs, then in egg, and again in crumbs; fry in deep fat and drain on brown paper.

### Cheese Aigrettes.

INGREDIENTS.

- ½ a cup of water.
- ¼ a cup of butter.
- ½ a cup of flour.
- 2 eggs, with yolk of a third.
- A few grains of cayenne and salt.
- 2 ounces (¼ a cup) of grated Parmesan cheese.
- Hot fat.

*Method.*—Boil the water and butter, sift in the flour with the salt and cayenne; stir and cook until the mixture cleaves from the side of the pan. When the mixture has slightly cooled, add the eggs, one at a time, beating in each egg thoroughly before another is added. Lastly, add the cheese. Drop, by teaspoonfuls, into hot fat and fry a golden brown. Drain on soft paper and serve piled on a folded napkin.

### Cheese d'Artois.

INGREDIENTS.

- 2 tablespoonfuls of butter.
- White of 1 egg.
- Yolks of 2 eggs.
- Salt and paprica.
- 2 ounces of grated Parmesan cheese.
- ¼ a pound of plain or puff paste.

*Method.*—Cream the butter, beat in the eggs, and add the cheese with a few grains, each, of salt and paprica. Roll the pastry very thin and cut it into two rectangular pieces; lay one of these on a baking-sheet and spread with the cheese mixture; cover this with the second piece of pastry. Score with a knife in strips one inch wide and about three inches long, brush over with beaten egg, and bake about fifteen minutes. Cut out the strips while hot. Serve at once, or reheat before serving.

**Pineapple Cheese and Crackers.**

**Salad of Lettuce with Cheese and Vegetable Macedoine.**

## Cheese Fritters.

Slice thin half a dozen large tart apples (select apples that cook quickly), and prepare half as many thin slices of cheese. Beat up one or two eggs, and season with salt, mustard and pepper. Soak the cheese in the egg mixture, then put each slice between two slices of apple, sandwich style; dip in the beaten egg, sauté in hot butter, and serve hot.

## Salad of Lettuce with Cheese and Vegetable Macedoine.

Mix together a ten-cent cream cheese, a canned pimento (red) cut in tiny cubes, one-fourth a cup of small green string beans, cut in cubes, five olives, chopped fine, and enough cream to hold the mixture together. When thoroughly mixed, use a piece of paraffine or confectioner's paper to handle and give the mixture the original shape. Let stand in a cold place, wrapped in the paper, until ready to serve, then dispose in the centre of a salad dish, lined with lettuce leaves, dressed with French dressing. Slice the cheese with a silver knife before sending to table. At luncheon, mayonnaise may be served in a dish apart.

# SANDWICHES.

A pale young man, with feeble whiskers and a stiff white neckcloth, came walking down the lane *en sandwich*—having a lady, that is, on each arm.

—*Thackeray* ("*Vanity Fair*").

The term "sandwich," now applied to many a fanciful shaped and encased dainty, was formerly used in speaking of "two slices of bread with meat between." In this sense, the word had its origin, about the end of the eighteenth century, from the fact that the fourth Earl of Sandwich was so infatuated with the pleasures and excitement of the gaming-table that he often could not leave it long enough to take his meals with his family; and, on such occasions, a butler was despatched to him bearing "slices of bread with meat between."

The fillings of savory sandwiches may be placed between pieces of bread, crackers, pastry, *chou* paste or aspic jelly. When preparing sweet sandwiches, these same materials may be used, as also lady-fingers (white or yellow), macaroons or sweet wafers.

## Bread for Sandwiches.

As a rule, bread for sandwiches should be twenty-four hours old; but fresh bread, which is more pliable than stale, is better adapted to this use, when the sandwiches are to take the form of rolls or folds. When stale bread is used for rolls or folds, they must be ribbon-tied; or tiny Japanese toothpicks may be made to keep them in shape.

The bread may be yeast or peptic bread. It may be white or brown. It is not even essential that the two bits of bread be of the same kind; Quaker, rice, whole-wheat, rye or graham bread is interchangeable with white or brown bread. After selecting your loaf or loaves, slice in even, quarter-inch slices; then cut in squares, triangles or fingers, or stamp with a round or fanciful-shaped cutter. Cutters can be obtained in heart, club, diamond and spade shape, also in racquet shape.

Do not spread butter or filling upon the bread before it is cut from the loaf and into shape. When so treated, the butter or filling on the extreme edge of the bread is liable to soil the fingers or gloves that come in contact with it.

Cream the butter, using a small wooden spoon for the purpose, and then it can be spread upon the most delicate bread without crumbling.

## The Filling.

Anything appropriately eaten with the *covering* may be used for the *filling* of a sandwich. In meats, salted meat takes the lead in popular favor; when sliced the meat should be cut across the grain and as thin as possible, and several bits should be used in each sandwich, unless a very small, æsthetic sandwich be in order. Tongue and corned beef, whether they be used in slices or finely chopped, should be cooked until they are very tender. When corned beef or ham is chopped for a filling, the sandwich is much improved by a dash of mustard; Worcestershire or horseradish sauce improves a filling of roast beef or boiled tongue; while chopped capers, tomato sauce, catsup or a cold mint sauce is appropriate in sandwiches made of lamb; celery salt, when the filling is of chicken or veal, and lemon juice, when the principal ingredient is fish, are *en rapport*.

The flavor of a few drops of onion juice is relished by many in any kind of fish or meat sandwich, while others would prefer a few grains of fine-chopped parsley.

When salad sandwiches are to be prepared, chop the meat or fish very fine and mix it with the salad dressing. Celery, cabbage, cress, cucumbers, tomatoes or olives may be chopped and added to the meat with the dressing. When lettuce is used, the leaf is served whole, the edges just appearing outside the bread. Any one of these vegetables, combined with a salad dressing, makes a delicious sandwich without meat or fish. When desired, other well-prepared sauces may be used in the place of salad dressings. Fillings of uncooked fruit may be used; but, in the case of dried fruits, it is preferable to stew until tender, after the fruit has been finely chopped. Pineapple, lemon or orange juice may be added at pleasure. Sandwiches prepared from entire-wheat bread, with fig or date fillings, are particularly wholesome for the children's luncheon basket.

When a particularly æsthetic sandwich is desired, wrap the butter that is to be used in spreading the bread in a napkin, and put it over night in a jar, on a bed of violets or rose petals; strew more flowers over the top and cover the jar tightly. If meat or fish is to be used as the basis of the sandwich, substitute nasturtium leaves and blossoms, or sprigs of mignonette, for the former flowers.

Fancy butter makes an attractive filling for a sandwich; it has also the merit of being less often in evidence than many another filling.

Sandwiches, except when vegetables and dressings are used, may be prepared early in the day, placed in a stone jar, covered with a slightly dampened cloth, and set away in a cool place until such time as they are wanted. Or, they may be wrapped in paraffine paper. Still, when convenient, it is preferable to have everything in readiness, and put the sandwiches together just before serving. Garnish the serving-dish with parsley, cress, celery plumes, slices of lemon, barberries and leaves, or fresh nasturtium leaves and blossoms.

## Beverages Served with Sandwiches.

Coffee heads the list of beverages most acceptably served with sandwiches. Tea comes next. Cocoa and chocolate are admissible only with the dainty, æsthetic varieties, in which fruit or some kind of sweetmeat is used.

*"Hail, wedded nourishment!"*

### Ham=and=Tongue Sandwiches.

Chop two parts of cold tongue and one part of cold ham (one-fourth as much fat ham as lean) very fine; pound in a mortar, and season with paprica and a little mixed mustard. Spread butter on one piece of bread, the meat mixture on the other, and press the two pieces together.

### Ham=and=Egg Sandwiches.

Chop the ham and pound smooth in a mortar; pass the yolks of hard-boiled eggs through a sieve; mix the yolks with an equal amount of mayonnaise dressing. Butter one piece of bread lightly and spread with the ham, spread the other piece with the egg and dressing, and press the two together.

### Corned=Beef Sandwiches.

Chop the cold meat very fine, using one-fourth of fat meat. Work into the meat French mustard, or any "made" mustard, to taste, and prepare the sandwiches in the usual way. Boston brownbread combines well with this preparation.

### Tongue=and=Veal (or Chicken) Sandwiches.

Use a little less of the chopped tongue than of the other kind of meat, and one-half as much chopped celery as meat. Mix with salad dressing. Spread one piece of bread with butter, the other with the mixture, and press together.

## Celery Sandwiches.

Chop crisp celery very fine and mix with salad dressing. Spread one piece of bread with butter, the other with a thin layer of the mixture. With a sharp knife split open the round stems of celery tips and put them between the bread, so that the tips will just show on the edges. Tie with narrow ribbon, light-green in color.

## Sardine Sandwiches.

Use, in bulk, equal parts of yolks of well-cooked eggs, rubbed to a smooth paste, and the flesh of sardines, freed from skin and bones and pounded in a mortar; season to taste with a few drops of tobasco sauce and lemon juice, and spread as usual. Crackers may be used in the place of bread, if the sandwiches be prepared just before using, otherwise the crackers lose their crispness. Garnish with slices of lemon and parsley.

## Caviare Sandwich Rolls.

To each two tablespoonfuls of caviare add ten drops of onion juice and a few drops of lemon juice, and mix together thoroughly. Remove the crust from a fresh, moist loaf of bread, cut in thin slices, spread each slice very delicately with butter and the caviare mixture, roll up in a roll and tie with ribbon one-fourth an inch wide, or pin with Chinese toothpicks. The bread should not be more than twelve hours old. If fear be lest the bread will not be sufficiently moist to roll, wrap the loaf, when taken from the oven, in a damp cloth and then in a dry one; keep in this fashion until ready for use.

## Russian Sandwiches.

Slightly butter thin slices of bread; moisten fine-chopped olives with mayonnaise dressing and spread upon the buttered slices; spread other slices with Neufchatel, or any cream cheese, and press together in pairs.

## Mushroom=and=Lobster Sandwiches.

Sauté the caps of half a pound of mushrooms in a little butter about five minutes, adding half a sliced onion if desired. Cover with highly seasoned stock and let simmer until very tender; chop and press through a sieve, and, if very moist, reduce to the consistency of a thick purée. Add an equal quantity of lobster meat pounded smooth in a mortar. Season to taste with salt, pepper, lemon juice and, if desired, tomato catsup. When cool use as any filling.

## Cheese=and=English=Walnut Sandwiches.

INGREDIENTS.

- ¼ a pound of grated cheese.
- ¼ a pound of butter.
- ¼ a pound of English walnut meats, sliced.
- Salt and paprica to taste.

*Method.*—Work the butter to a cream, add the seasonings and the grated cheese gradually; then mix in the nuts, which should be *sliced* very thin.

Spread the mixture upon bits of bread and press together in pairs. Particularly good made of brownbread and served with a simple vegetable salad!

### Egg=and=Spinach Sandwiches.

Use cold boiled spinach, which when hot was chopped very fine or pressed through a colander, and sifted yolks of well-cooked eggs. Mix the spinach with sauce tartare and spread on one bit of bread, spread the other with butter and sifted yolk of egg; press together. Garnish the serving-dish with parsley and cooked eggs cut in quarters lengthwise.

### Cress=and=Egg Sandwiches.

Pick the leaves from fresh cress, chop or break apart, season with French dressing, and proceed as above.

### Imitation Pâté=de=Foie=Gras Sandwiches.

Chop half an onion and sauté in a little butter; when delicately browned, add five or six chicken livers and sauté them on both sides. Cover with well-seasoned chicken stock and let simmer until tender. Mash the livers fine with a wooden spoon and press them through a sieve; season with salt, paprica, mustard, or a dash of curry powder. Press into a cup, pour melted butter over the top, and set away in a cool place. When ready to serve, remove the butter and prepare the sandwiches after the usual manner.

## Chicken Rolls.

### Ingredients.

- 4 ounces from the breast of chicken (½ a cup).
- 4 ounces of braised tongue.
- ½ a teaspoonful of celery salt.
- A few grains of cayenne.
- 1 teaspoonful of anchovy paste.
- 4 tablespoonfuls of mayonnaise or boiled dressing.

*Method.*—Chop the meat and pound to a paste in a mortar; add the seasonings and mix well. Remove the crust from a loaf of moist bread; cut in very thin slices, trim each slice into a rectangular shape, spread lightly with soft butter and then with the mixture. Roll the slices and tie them with ribbon. Omit the anchovy paste, if desired.

## Epicurean Sandwiches.

Cream four tablespoonfuls of butter and one teaspoonful of mustard. Press the yolks of four hard-boiled eggs through a sieve and add them to the butter and mustard. Then add four boned anchovies, four small pickles, a teaspoonful of chives and a sprig of tarragon, chopped together until fine. Cut stale bread in fingers or other fanciful shapes, and spread with the mixture. Press two pieces together.

## Halibut=and=Lettuce Sandwiches.

Put a pound and a half of halibut, a slice of onion, a stalk of celery, four or five peppercorns, one teaspoonful of salt and one tablespoonful of lemon juice in boiling water, and cook, just below the boiling-point, ten or fifteen minutes, according to thickness. Remove bone and skin and rub the fish fine with a wooden spoon; add half a cup of thick cream, a teaspoonful of salt, a dash of white pepper and one tablespoonful of lemon juice. Spread this mixture, when cold, on buttered slices of bread, put a lettuce leaf above the mixture, and spread a teaspoonful of mayonnaise or boiled salad dressing on the lettuce; finish with a slice of buttered bread and tie with ribbon.

## Lobster Fingers.

Chop lobster meat very fine; season to taste with French dressing. Cut the bread in pieces about four inches long and an inch and a half wide. Finish as usual. Garnish with parsley and the slender feelers of the lobster.

## Tower of Babel.

Pile a *variety* of sandwiches in form of a pyramid (use bread of different colors). Arrange a garnish of parsley and radish rosebuds around the base, and on the top a few sprigs of parsley, or celery plumes.

## Nasturtium Folds.

Flavor the butter with nasturtium leaves and blossoms, and with it spread a thin slice of *moist* bread, which is longer one way than the other. Press fresh nasturtium leaves and blossoms upon the butter and fold one half over the other.

## Harlequin Sandwiches.

Spread a bit of brownbread with butter and French mustard, and a bit of white bread, cut to fit the former, with butter and cheese creamed together. Finish as usual.

### Harlequin Sandwiches, No. 2.

Spread the brownbread with butter and cheese creamed together, and the white bread with butter, then with cucumber, chopped fine and seasoned with French dressing, to which a few drops of onion juice have been added.

### Beet=and=Cream=Cheese Sandwiches.

Spread one piece of bread with cream cheese, the other with beets that have been chopped very fine and seasoned with French dressing.

### Peanut Sandwiches.

Chop freshly roasted peanuts very fine; then pound them in a mortar until smooth; season with salt and moisten with thick cream.

### Chicken Salad Sandwiches.
See page 127

**Halibut Sandwiches with Aspic.**
See page 128

## Peanut Sandwiches, No. 2.

Mix the prepared peanuts with mayonnaise dressing. Butter two pieces of bread; spread one with the peanut mixture, the other with shredded lettuce, and press the two together.

## Shad=Roe=and=Yellow=Butter Sandwiches.

INGREDIENTS.

- ¼ a pound of butter.
- Sifted yolks of 4 eggs.
- 1 set of shad roe, cooked, pounded in a mortar and sifted.
- ½ a teaspoonful of paprica.
- 4 drops of tobasco sauce.
- 2 teaspoonfuls of very fine-chopped capers.

*Method.*—Cream the butter and add the other ingredients gradually. Prepare as usual.

## Green=Butter Sandwiches.

INGREDIENTS.

- ¼ a pound of butter.
- 1/8 a peck of spinach.
- 2 tablespoonfuls of very fine-chopped parsley.
- 6 anchovies.
- 2 teaspoonfuls of very fine-chopped capers.

*Method.*—Boil the spinach, drain thoroughly, and press through a piece of muslin. Beat the butter to a cream with a wooden spoon; beat into the butter enough of the spinach pulp to give the required tint of green. Wipe the oil from the anchovies, remove the backbone, and pass through a hair sieve; then add to the colored butter, a little at a time; add also the parsley and capers; chill slightly and use as a filling for sandwiches. These butters are used also to mask or decorate cooked fish for "cold service."

## Chicken=Salad Sandwiches.

(*Chou-paste boxes.*)

(See cut facing [page 126](page 126).)

Bake *chou* paste in long, slender shapes, like éclairs, but narrower and shorter; when cold split apart on the ends and one side and fill with chicken salad. Put the top back in place, after inserting a celery plume at each end. Garnish the serving-dish with celery leaves and pim-olas or olives. Serve other salads in the same way.

## Mosaic Sandwiches.

Cut the bread, white, brown and graham, as thin as possible, and use four or five pieces in each sandwich, putting them together so that the colors will contrast. Either butter or other filling is admissible.

### Chicken=and=Nut Sandwiches.

Chop fine the white meat of a cooked chicken and pound to a paste in a mortar. Season to taste with salt, paprica, oil and lemon juice and spread upon thin bits of bread. Spread other bits of bread, corresponding in shape to the first, with butter; press into the butter English walnuts, pecan nuts or almonds, blanched and *sliced* very thin. Press corresponding pieces together.

### Aspic Jelly for Sandwiches.

Soak one box (two ounces) of gelatine in one cup of cold chicken liquor until thoroughly softened. Add to three cups of chicken stock, seasoned with vegetables and sweet herbs according to directions previously given, also the crushed shell and white of one egg, and proceed as for aspic jelly. Turn the liquid jelly into rectangular pans, having it three-eighths of an inch or less in thickness, and set aside in a cool place to harden. When ready to serve, dip the pan in hot water an instant, and turn the jelly on to a paper. With a thin, sharp knife cut the jelly into squares or diamonds, or dip a cutter into hot water and stamp out into hearts or clubs.

### Lobster Sandwiches with Aspic.

Chop the lobster fine, mix with mayonnaise dressing to taste, spread upon a bit of aspic, cover with a crisp lettuce leaf, and above this place another piece of aspic spread with the lobster mixture. Serve at once.

## Halibut Sandwiches with Aspic.

After the aspic is poured into the pans, sprinkle upon it some fine-cut Spanish pimentos. When ready to serve, prepare as lobster sandwiches with aspic, using fish in the place of lobster, and, if desired, sauce tartare in the place of mayonnaise. Shrimps, salmon or other fish, chicken, veal, tongue, sweetbreads, etc., may be used either with lettuce or with chopped celery, cress, cucumbers, etc. Or the vegetables may be used without either fish, flesh or fowl.

**Wedding Sandwich Rolls.**
See page 129

**Club Sandwich.**
See page 129

## Club Sandwiches.

(*Steamer Priscilla style.*)

Have ready four triangular pieces of toasted bread spread with mayonnaise dressing; cover two of these with lettuce, lay thin slices of cold chicken (white meat) upon the lettuce, over this arrange slices of broiled breakfast bacon, then lettuce, and cover with the other triangles of toast spread with mayonnaise. Trim neatly, arrange on a plate, and garnish with heart leaves of lettuce dipped in mayonnaise.

## Wedding Sandwich Rolls.

Wrap bread as it is taken from the oven closely in a towel wrung out of cold water, cover with several thicknesses of dry cloth and set aside about four hours; then cut away the crust, and with a thin, sharp knife cut the loaf or loaves in slices as thin as possible and spread with butter, and, if desired, thin shavings of meat, potted meat or chopped nuts; roll the slices very closely and pile on a serving-dish.

## The Milwaukee Sandwich.

### Ingredients.

- 2 thin rounds of white bread.
- 1 thin round of graham or rye bread.
- 4 large oysters, broiled or fried.
- Breast of cooked chicken, or turkey.
- Two slices of crisp bacon.
- Horseradish.
- Lettuce.
- 4 small sweet pickles.
- 4 small radishes.
- Slice of lemon.
- 1 tomato, skin removed.
- Tartare sauce.

*Method.*—Dip the bread in beaten egg, seasoned with salt and sauté to a rich brown in hot butter. Roll the oysters in grated bread crumbs (centre of the loaf) and broil them, or "egg and bread" them, and fry in deep fat. Lay the first slice of bread on a plate over two or three lettuce leaves, put the oysters on the bread, a grating of horseradish on each oyster; cover with the graham or rye bread; on this lay the chicken or turkey cut in thin slices, season with salt and pepper, put on the bacon, and cover with the other slice of bread. On top of the sandwich lay a slice of lemon cut square, and about this dispose the pickles and radishes, to form a star. Serve the tomato on a lettuce leaf at the side. Cut out the hard centre from the tomato and fill the opening with sauce tartare. In making this sauce, add to mayonnaise or boiled dressing, onion, olives, sweet pickles and celery, chopped fine and squeezed dry in a cloth.

# SWEET SANDWICHES.

In the name of the Prophet—figs!
—*Horace Smith.*

## Fig Sandwiches.

Chop one-fourth a pound of figs very fine, add one-fourth a cup of water, and cook to a smooth paste; add, also, one-third a cup of almonds, blanched, chopped very fine and pounded to a paste with a little rose-water, also the juice of half a lemon. When cold spread the mixture upon lady-fingers or cakelets, white or yellow, press another above the mixture, and serve upon a handsome doylie-covered plate. Raisins, dates or marmalade may be used in the place of the figs. The marmalade, of course, requires no cooking. Bread may be used in the place of the cake.

## French Fruit Sandwiches.

Chop the fruit very fine; use a mixture of cherries, plums, pineapple and angelica root; moisten with wine, orange or lemon juice. Use lady-fingers or bread for the covering. If bread is used, spread lightly with butter; if cake be your choice, spread very lightly with marmalade. Use just enough butter or marmalade to keep the coverings together.

## Date=and=Ginger Sandwiches.

Chop the dates and preserved ginger; moisten with syrup from the ginger jar and a little lemon juice; cook as above, and use with bread or lady-fingers. Preserved ginger may be used alone and without cooking.

### Rose=Leaf Sandwiches.

Flavor the butter with rose petals according to the directions previously given. Spread both bits of bread lightly with it and put upon them three or four candied rose petals. If lady-fingers are used, brush them over with white of egg and sugar mixed together. Use but little sugar—just enough to hold the fingers together. The Turkish rose petals that come in little jars are particularly dainty, and adapted to this purpose. Garnish the dish on which they are served with rosebuds and leaves.

### Violet Sandwiches.

Prepare in the same manner as in the last number, substituting candied violets for the rose petals, and violets with green leaves for a garnish.

### Honey Sandwiches.

Spread one bit of white bread with honey pressed from the comb with a wooden spoon, the other bit with butter. Garnish with white clover blossoms and leaves.

### Puff=Paste Sandwiches.

Roll puff paste very thin (about one-eighth of an inch), cut in fanciful shapes and bake to a delicate brown; add chopped almonds to rich strawberry preserves, or peach marmalade, and spread the mixture between each two bits of pastry.

## Pineapple Sandwiches.

### Ingredients.

- 1 cup of pineapple juice and pulp.
- ¾ a cup of sugar.
- Juice of half a lemon.
- Lady-fingers.

*Method.*—Cook the pineapple, sugar and lemon juice until thick; let cool, and spread upon lady-fingers or sponge drops. Press together in pairs and serve.

## Whipped=Cream Sandwiches.

### Ingredients.

- 1 cup of heavy cream.
- ¼ a cup of powdered sugar.
- ¼ a teaspoonful of vanilla extract.
- Lady-fingers.

*Method.*—Add the sugar and extract to the cream and beat until solid; let chill, then spread quite thick upon lady-fingers or sponge drops.

## Whipped=Cream Sandwiches with French Fruit.

Soak half a cup of fine-cut candied fruit in wine an hour or more. Prepare the cream as above, and sprinkle the same with the fruit before putting the sandwiches together.

## Fruit Jelly for Sweet Sandwiches.

INGREDIENTS.

- 1 box of gelatine (2 ounces).
- 1 cup of cold water.
- 1 cup of boiling water.
- 1 cup of sugar.
- 1½ cups of orange juice.
- ¼ a cup of lemon juice.

*Method.*—Soak the gelatine in the cold water and dissolve in the boiling water; add the sugar and strain; when cold add the orange and lemon juice. Mould in sheets three-eighths of an inch thick.

## Claret Jelly for Sweet Sandwiches.

Substitute claret for the orange juice and prepare as above. Do not omit the lemon juice.

## Fruit or Claret Jelly Sandwiches with Nuts.

Slice blanched English walnuts and pecan nuts or almonds very thin, and stir into whipped cream. Stamp out shapes from the jelly. Spread one piece with the cream and nuts and cover with a second piece of jelly.

## With French Fruit.

Substitute candied fruit for the nuts and proceed as above, or use nuts and fruit together.

## Cupid's Butter Sandwiches.

Ingredients.

- The yolks of 4 hard-boiled eggs.
- 1 cup of butter.
- 1/3 a cup of powdered sugar.
- 1 teaspoonful of orange juice.
- A grating of orange rind.
- Angel cakelets or slices of angel cake.

*Method.*—Cream the butter, gradually add the yolks of eggs, passed through a potato ricer or sieve, the sugar and orange juice. Spread upon thin slices of angel cake, prepared for sandwiches, or upon angel cakelets or fingers; press two slices together and serve at once. If allowed to stand any length of time, keep covered and in a cool place.

## Cheese=and=Bar=le=Duc Currant Sandwiches.

Spread wheat bread, prepared for sandwiches, with cream cheese; put two or three currants and a little syrup on each piece of bread, and press two pieces together. These may be varied by using sliced maraschino cherries. Either the currants or sliced cherries with a little of the syrup may be mixed with the cheese and then spread upon the bread. Bar-le-Duc currants are imported from France in tiny glasses. The seeds have been removed from the currants, which are cooked in honey.

### Hunter's Sandwich (Switzerland).

Spread fresh bread, cut in thin slices, with fresh butter; over this spread a layer of Brie or other cream cheese, and over the cheese spread a layer of honey. Press two similarly shaped pieces together and serve at once.

### Hunter's Sandwich (Ellwanger).

Prepare as above, substituting maple syrup (or sugar) for the honey.

# BREAD AND CHOU PASTE.

She needeth least, who kneadeth best,
These rules which we shall tell;
Who kneadeth ill shall need them more
Than she who kneadeth well.
—F.F.

## Two Loaves of Wheat Bread.

To two cups of scalded milk or boiled water, in a mixing-bowl, add two tablespoonfuls of sugar, one teaspoonful of salt, and, when the liquid becomes lukewarm, one yeastcake dissolved in half a cup of water, boiled and cooled. With a broad-bladed knife cut and mix in enough well-dried flour, sifted, to make a stiff dough (about seven cups). Knead until the dough is elastic; cover, and set to rise in a temperature of about 70° Fahr. When the dough has doubled in bulk, "cut down" and knead slightly without removing from the mixing-bowl. When again double in bulk, shape into two double loaves and set to rise in buttered pans; when it has risen a third time, bake one hour.

## Entire=Wheat Bread.

Use the preceding recipe without change other than in kind of flour and two additional tablespoonfuls of sugar.

**Boston Brown Bread.**

**Bread cut for Sandwiches.**

## Rice Bread.

Add three-fourths a cup of rice, cooked until tender and still hot, and, also, two tablespoonfuls of butter, to the milk or water in the first recipe. Other cereals, as oatmeal or cerealine, may be used instead of rice.

## Salad Rolls.

Make a sponge with one cup of milk, one yeastcake dissolved in one-fourth a cup of milk, and about one cup and a half of flour; beat thoroughly, cover, and set to rise in a temperature of about 70° Fahr. When light add half a teaspoonful of salt, one-fourth a cup of melted butter, and flour enough to knead. Knead until elastic. Set to rise in a temperature of 70° Fahr. When doubled in bulk, cut down and shape into small balls. Set to rise again, covered with a cloth and a dripping-pan. When light press the handle of a small wooden spoon deeply across the centre of each ball, brush with butter and press the edges together. Set the rolls close together in a baking-pan, after brushing over with butter the points of contact.

## Boston Brownbread.

Sift together one cup, each, of yellow corn meal, rye meal and entire-wheat flour, one teaspoonful of salt and three teaspoonfuls of soda. Add three-fourths a cup of molasses and one pint of thick, sour milk. Beat thoroughly, and steam in a covered mould three hours and a half. The quantity here given may be steamed in four baking-powder boxes in two hours.

## Baking=Powder Biscuit.

Pass through the sieve two or three times four cups of flour, one teaspoonful of salt, and, for each cup of flour, two level teaspoonfuls of baking-powder. With the tips of the fingers work into the flour one-third a cup of butter. When the mixture looks like meal, mix in gradually nearly one pint of milk, cutting the dough with a knife until well mixed. When it is of a consistency to handle, turn out on to a well-floured board, toss with the knife in the flour, then pat out into a sheet half an inch thick, and cut into rounds. Let the heat of the oven be moderate at first, and increase after the dough has risen. Bake about fifteen minutes.

## Sandwich Biscuit.

Prepare the dough as above, roll to about three-eighths an inch in thickness, and cut into rounds. Spread one half of these with softened butter, and press the others, unbuttered, upon them; bake fifteen or eighteen minutes.

## Pulled Bread.

(*To serve with simple salads and cheese.*)

Remove the crust from a fresh loaf of French bread. Gash the loaf at the ends and pull apart into halves; then cut the halves and pull apart into quarters. Repeat until the pieces are about the thickness of breadsticks. Put on a rack in a dripping-pan, and dry out the moisture in a slow oven; then brown delicately. Keep in a dry place (a tin box is suitable) and reheat in the oven before serving.

## How to Give Rolls and Bread a Glossy, Brown Crust.

A short time before removing from the oven, brush over the top of each loaf or roll with beaten yolk of egg, diluted with a little milk, or with a little sugar dissolved in milk, or with thin starch.

## Chou Paste.

Put a saucepan with half a cup of butter and one cup of boiling water over the fire. When the mixture boils, beat into it one cup of flour. When the dough cleaves from the sides of the saucepan, turn into a bowl and beat in, one at a time, three large or four small eggs.

---

## To Boil Salted Meats: Ham, Tongue, Etc.

Cover the meat with cold water and bring the water slowly to the boiling-point; let boil five minutes, then *slightly* bubble until the meat is tender.

## To Boil Chicken, Lamb and Other Fresh Meat.

Cover the meat with boiling water, let boil rapidly five minutes, then keep the water just below the boiling-point, or just "quivering" at one side of the saucepan, until the meat is tender. When the meat is about half cooked, add a teaspoonful of salt for each quart of water.

## Potted Meat and Fish for Sandwiches.

### Ingredients.

- 1 pound of tender cooked meat or fish (2 cups).
- 2 ounces of fat cooked meat (¼ a cup).
- 2 ounces of butter (¼ a cup).
- Mace and anchovy essence, if desired.
- Pepper and salt.

*Method.*—Chop the meat or fish very fine, then pass through a purée sieve; cream the butter and with a wooden spoon work it into the meat or fish; add seasonings to taste, press the mixture solidly into small jars or cups, and pour melted butter to the depth of one-fourth an inch over the top of the meat. Set aside in a cool place.

## Kinds of Meat and Fish for Potting.

Ham, fat and lean; either chicken, veal or tongue, with bacon; chicken and ham, mixed, fat ham; chicken and tongue, mixed, with bacon; veal and ham, mixed, with fat ham; roast beef and corned beef, mixed, with fat of either, or bacon; finnan-haddie and bacon; salmon, cod, haddock, bluefish, etc., with bacon, or with double the amount of butter.

**Bowl of Fruit-Punch Ready for Serving.**

# BEVERAGES SERVED WITH SANDWICHES.

> Towards eve there was tea
> (A luxury due to Matilda) and ice,
> Fruit and coffee.
> —*Meredith's "Lucile."*
>
> Come, touch to your lips this melting sweetness,
> Sip of this nectar,—this Java fine,—
> Whose tawny drops hold more completeness
> Than lurks in the depths of ruby wine.
> —*J. M. L.*

## Filtered Coffee.

INGREDIENTS.

- ½ a cup of coffee, ground very fine.
- 3 cups of boiling water.
- About 6 blocks of sugar.
- About 3 tablespoonfuls of cream.
- About 6 tablespoonfuls of hot milk.

*Method.*—Put the coffee into the filter of a well-scalded coffee-pot. Pour the boiling water over the coffee. Serve as soon as the infusion has dripped through the filter. For black coffee use double the quantity of coffee.

## Boiled Coffee.

INGREDIENTS.

- 1 cup of ground coffee.
- White and shell of 1 egg.
- 1 cup of cold water.
- 6 cups of boiling water.
- 1 tablespoonful of ground coffee.

*Method.*—Beat the white and crushed shell of the egg and half the cup of cold water together; mix with the coffee, pour over the boiling water, stir thoroughly, and boil from three to five minutes with the nozzle tightly closed; pour half a cup of cold water down the spout; stir in one tablespoonful of coffee and let stand on the range, without boiling, ten minutes.

## Five=o'clock Tea.

INGREDIENTS.

- Tea.
- Candied ox-heart cherries.
- Slices of lemon.
- Boiling water.

*Method.*—Fill the tea-ball half full with tea, put the ball into the cup, with a cherry or a slice of lemon, and pour boiling water over them; remove the ball when the tea is of the desired strength.

## Rich Chocolate.

INGREDIENTS.

- 4 ounces of chocolate.

- 4 tablespoonfuls of granulated sugar.
- ¼ a cup of hot water.
- 1 quart of scalded milk.
- 1 teaspoonful of vanilla extract.
- Whites of 3 eggs.
- 1 pint of thick cream.
- 1/3 a cup of powdered sugar.

*Method.*—Grate the chocolate, add the granulated sugar and hot water, and cook until smooth and glossy; with a whisk beat in the hot milk very gradually, and return to a double boiler to keep hot. Beat the cream until solid. Beat the whites of the eggs until dry, then beat in the powdered sugar and fold the cream into the egg and sugar. Add half of the cream mixture to the chocolate with the vanilla, and mix while the cream is heating. Serve the rest of the cream in spoonfuls upon the chocolate in the cups.

## Plain Chocolate.

Prepare as in preceding recipe, omitting the cream mixture and such portion of the chocolate as is desired.

## Plain Cocoa.

INGREDIENTS.

- 4 teaspoonfuls of cocoa.
- 4 teaspoonfuls of sugar.
- 1 cup of boiling water,
- 1 cup of hot milk.
- Whipped cream, if desired.

*Method.*—Mix the cocoa and sugar, pour over the boiling water, and when boiling again add the hot milk; beat the whipped cream into the hot cocoa, or serve a spoonful upon the top of each cup.

## Ceylon Cocoa.

Scald a two-inch piece of paper-bark cinnamon with the milk to be used in making the cocoa.

## Sultana Cocoa.

Stem and wash half a pound of sultana raisins; let them stand, covered with one quart of boiling water, upon the back of the range an hour or more; filter the water through folds of cheese-cloth and use in making cocoa or chocolate.

## Egg Lemonade.

INGREDIENTS.

- 1 egg.
- 4 tablespoonfuls of sugar.
- Juice of 2 lemons.
- 2 cups of water.

*Method.*—Beat the egg until white and yolk are well mixed; then beat in the sugar, the lemon juice and the water.

## Fruit Punch.

Ingredients.

- 1 pineapple.
- 4 cups of sugar.
- 3 cups of boiling water.
- 1 cup of tea, freshly made.
- 5 lemons.
- 6 oranges.
- 1 pint of strawberry or grape juice.
- ½ a pint of maraschino cherries.
- 1 bottle of Apollinaris water.
- 6 quarts of water.

*Method.*—Grate the pineapple, add the boiling water and the sugar, and boil fifteen minutes; add the tea and strain into the punch-bowl. When cold add the fruit juice, the cherries and the cold water. A short time before serving, add a piece of ice, and, on serving, the Apollinaris water. Strawberries, mint leaves, or slices of banana may be used in the place of the cherries.

## Punch à la Nantes.

Ingredients.

- 2 pounds of rhubarb.
- 1 pint of water.
- 1 bay leaf.
- 1 cup of sugar.
- 1 cup of orange juice.
- ¼ a cup of lemon juice.
- ¼ a cup of ginger syrup.

*Method.*—Cut the rhubarb into pieces without peeling; add the bay leaf and water, and let simmer until the rhubarb is tender; strain through a cheese-cloth. Boil the juice with the sugar five minutes. When cold add the orange and lemon juice, with one-fourth a cup of syrup from a jar of preserved ginger, and a piece of ice. Add water as needed.

## Home=made Soda Water.

Ingredients.

- 2¼ pounds of granulated sugar.
- 1¾ ounces of tartaric acid.
- 1 pint of water.
- Whites of 3 eggs.
- ½ an ounce of ginger extract.
- ¼ a teaspoonful of bicarbonate of soda for each glass.

*Method.*—Boil the sugar, water and tartaric acid five minutes. When nearly cold beat into the syrup the whites of the eggs, beaten until foamy, and the flavoring extract. Store in a fruit jar, closely covered. To use, put three tablespoonfuls into a glass half full of cold water, stir in one-fourth a teaspoonful of soda, and drink while effervescing. A pint of any kind of fruit juice may displace the water, when a teaspoonful of lemon juice should be added to the contents of each glass before stirring in the soda.

## Spanish Chocolate.

(*To serve 60.*)

Ingredients.

- 6 quarts of milk.
- 3 blades of mace.
- 1 five-inch stick of cinnamon.
- 12 cloves.
- 20 pounded almonds.
- 1 pound of chocolate.
- 3 cups of sugar.
- 2 quarts of boiling water.
- Yolks of three eggs.

*Method.*—Scald the milk with the spices and nuts. Break up the chocolate and melt over hot water; add the sugar, mix thoroughly, then gradually stir in the boiling water; let cook two or three minutes after all the water has been added, then turn into the hot milk; let stand over hot water until ready to serve, then add the beaten yolks of eggs, diluted with half a cup of water, milk or cream, and strain through a cheese-cloth. Keep hot over hot water.

## Claret Cup.

Ingredients.

- 2 quarts of claret.
- 1 cup of sugar.
- 1 cup of water.
- 5 lemons cut in slices.
- 1 dozen whole cloves.
- 2 qts. of charged Apollinaris or soda water.
- ¼ a cup of brandy, sherry or maraschino.
- Ice.

Boil the sugar and water about six minutes; let cool, then add the lemon slices, with seeds removed, and the cloves; let stand some hours in a cold place. When ready to serve, add the claret, water and liqueur, all chilled on ice. Put a piece of ice in the pitcher and pour over it the mixture. The beverage should not be sweet.

**Copper Chafing-Dish with Earthen Casserole.**

# Chafing=dishes Past and Present.

*Well, he was an ingenious man that first found out eating and drinking.—*
*Swift.*

How fire was discovered, when it was first applied to the needs of human beings, the origin and early use of cooking and heating utensils,—all are concealed from us in the mists that surround the life of prehistoric man. But at the dawn of history, even before the beginning of our era, crude appliances for cooking were in use; and, without doubt, one of the earliest of these was an utensil corresponding in some particulars, at least, to the chafing-dish of to-day.

The chafing-dish is a portable utensil used upon the table, either for cooking food or for keeping food hot after it has been cooked by other means. In ancient times, the fuel of the chafing-dish was either live coals or olive oil; to-day we use either electricity, gas, alcohol or colonial spirits.

The first chafing-dishes of which historic mention is made consisted of a pan heated over a pot of burning oil, the pan resting upon a frame which held the pot of oil. It was with such an utensil, perhaps, that the Israelitish women cooked the locusts of Egypt and Palestine, for these were eaten as a common food by the people of the biblical lands and age.

Mommsen, in his history of Rome, while speaking of the extravagance of the times, as shown in the table furnishings, probably refers to the chafing-dish when he says: "A well-wrought bronze cooking-machine came to cost more than an estate." The idea that this might be the utensil referred to is strengthened by the fact that many chafing-dishes have been found in the ruins of Pompeii. These were made of bronze, and highly ornamented. Evidently, olive oil was the fuel used in these dishes.

Coming down to more modern times, Madame de Staël had a dish of very unique pattern, and, when driven by the command of Napoleon from her beloved Paris, she carried her chafing-dish with her into exile as one of her most cherished household gods. At the present day among the favored few, who have full purses, are found sets of little silver chafing-dishes about four inches square. These tiny dishes rest upon a doylie-covered plate, and a bird or rarebit may be served in them as a course at dinner, one to each guest. The cooking is not done in these dishes, and they are not furnished with lamps; in them the food, while it is being eaten, is simply kept hot by means of a tiny pan filled with hot water.

In reality, the modern chafing-dish is a species of *bain marie*, or double boiler, with a lamp so arranged that cooking can be done without other appliances. It consists of four parts. The *first* is the blazer, or the pan in which the cooking is done; this is provided with a long handle. The *second* is the hot-water pan, which corresponds to the lower part of the double boiler; this should be provided with handles, and is a very inconvenient dish without them. The *third* is the frame upon which the hot-water pan rests, and in which the spirit-lamp is set. The *last*, but by no means least, part is the lamp; this is provided with a cotton or an asbestos wick. When the lamp has a cotton wick, the flame is regulated by turning the wick up or down, as in an ordinary lamp. At present this style of lamp is found only in the more expensive grades of dishes,—silver-plated, and costing from $15 upwards. When asbestos is used as the wick, the lamp is filled with this porous stone, which is to be saturated with alcohol immediately before using, and the top is covered with a wire netting. The flame is regulated by means of metal slides, which open and shut over the netting, thus cutting off or letting on the flame, as it is desired.

**Chafing-Dish, Filler, Etc.**
"With all Appliances and Means to boot."

## Chafing=dish Appointments.

With all appliances and means to boot.
—Henry IV., iii. I.

The chafing-dish should always rest upon a tray, as a very slight draught of air, or the expansion of the alcohol when heated, will sometimes cause the flame to flare out and downward, and thus an unprotected tablecloth might be set on fire.

Often a cutlet dish is considered a necessary part of a chafing-dish outfit; but as one of the chief merits of the chafing-dish consists in the possibility of serving a repast the instant it is cooked, there would seem to be a want of propriety in removing the cooked article to a platter and garnishing the dish before serving.

A polished wooden spoon, with long handle and small bowl, is a most convenient utensil to use while cooking the dainty; but the regulation chafing-dish spoon is needed when serving the same. Such a spoon has a broad bowl of silver or aluminum, with rounded end, and a long ebony handle.

The filler is a most convenient article for use, when the lamp needs replenishing with alcohol, but in its absence the alcohol may be turned into a small pitcher and from that into the lamp. A lamp of the average size holds about five tablespoonfuls of alcohol, and this quantity will supply heat for at least half an hour.

Glass, granite or tin measuring-cups, upon which thirds or quarters are indicated, also tea- and tablespoons, are essential for accurate measurements.

Several items are essential to the successful serving of a meal from the chafing-dish. To be a pronounced success, the work must be done noiselessly and gracefully. The preparation of all articles is the same for the chafing-dish as for the common stove; but where the mixing is done at the table, as for a rarebit, the recipe takes on an additional flavor, according to the deftness with which it is done.

Let, then, everything be ready and at hand, before the guests or family assemble at the table. Have the lamp filled and covered, so that it may remain filled. Have all seasonings measured out in a cup. In case the yolks of eggs are to be used, they will not injure, having been beaten beforehand, if they be kept covered. When oysters are to be served, have them washed, freed from bits of shell, drained, and left in a pitcher from which they can be readily poured. The quantity of butter used in the recipes is indicated by tablespoonfuls, and may be measured out beforehand and rolled into dainty balls with butter-hands, a spoonful in each ball.

Bear in mind that the hot-water pan is to be used in all cases where the double boiler would be used, if the cooking were to be done upon the range. For instance, where the recipe calls for milk or cream, except in the making of a sauce, use the bath from the beginning. Also, be careful always to place the blazer in the bath before eggs are added to any mixture. Indeed, the hot-water pan is the one feature of the chafing-dish which it is most important to notice; for on the proper use of the hot-water pan the value of the chafing-dish as an exponent of scientific cookery entirely depends. She who well understands the principles upon which the use of this rests has gained no small insight into the secret of all cookery, be it scientific, economic or hygienic; for a knowledge of the effect of heat at different temperatures, applied to food, is the very foundation-stone upon which all cookery rests.

Although the chafing-dish is especially adapted to the needs of the bachelor, man or maid, its use should not be relegated entirely to the homeless or the Bohemian. In the sick-room, at the luncheon-table, on Sunday night, it is most serviceable and wellnigh indispensable; it always suggests hearty welcome and good cheer.

While it is out of place, at any ceremonial meal, as a means of cooking, even on such occasions a lobster Newburgh or other dish that needs be served piping hot to be eaten at its best may be brought on in individual chafing-dishes. These are supplied with hot-water pans and lamps. At a chafing-dish supper each guest can prepare his own rarebit.

Any operation in cooking that can be performed on the kitchen range may be successfully carried out on the chafing-dish, provided one be skilled in its use. But as the dining-room is usually chosen as the site in which to test its possibilities, here it were well to confine one's efforts to such dishes as will not give rise to too much disorder. Sautéing and frying it were better to reserve for the range and a well-ventilated kitchen.

Alcohol is most commonly used in the lamp of the chafing-dish; and, on account of its cheapness, one is often advised to buy *wood* alcohol. But in large markets, where many fowl are singed daily over an alcohol flame, the marketmen will tell you that the very best article is none too good for their purpose. It does not smoke, wastes less rapidly, and in the end will prove quite as economical.

**Course at Formal Dinner served in Individual Chafing-Dishes.**
See page 157

## Are Midnight Suppers Hygienic?

"Being no further enemy to you
  Than the constraint of hospitable zeal."

In regard to the chafing-dish and its most prominent use, some one may fittingly ask: Is it hygienic to eat at midnight? Can one keep one's health and eat late suppers? As in all things pertaining to food, no set rules can be given to meet every case; much depends upon constitutional traits, individual habits and idiosyncrasies. One may practise what another cannot attempt. As a rule, however, people who eat a hearty dinner, after the work of the day is done, do not need to eat again until the following breakfast hour.

Those who are engaged, either mentally or physically, throughout the evening, cannot with impunity, eat a very hearty meal previous to that effort; but after their work is done they need nourishing food, and food that is both easily digested and assimilated. But even these should not eat and then immediately retire; for during sleep all the bodily organs, including the stomach, become dormant. Food partaken at this hour is not properly taken care of, and in too many cases must be digested when the individual has awakened, out of sorts, the next morning.

It is well to remember, also, that, at any time after food is eaten, there should be a period of rest from all active effort; for then the blood flows from the other organs of the body to the stomach, and the work of digestion is begun. Oftentimes we hear men say they must smoke after meals, for unless they do so they cannot digest their food. They fail to see that it is not the tobacco that promotes digestion, but the enforced repose.

But, if we must eat at midnight, the question may well be asked, What shall we eat? That which can be digested and assimilated with the least effort on the part of the digestive organs. And among such things we may note oysters, eggs and game, when these have been properly—that is, delicately—cooked.

## How to Make Sauces.

Let hunger move thy appetyte, and not savory sauces.—*Babees Book.*

"Change is the sauce that sharpens appetite."

As so many dishes are prepared in the chafing-dish that require the use of a simple sauce, we give in this place the methods usually followed in the preparation of common sauces. For one cup of sauce, put two tablespoonfuls of butter into the blazer; let the butter simply melt, without coloring, if for a white sauce, but cook until brown for a brown sauce. Mix together two tablespoonfuls of flour, one-fourth a teaspoonful of salt and a dash of black or white pepper, or a few grains of cayenne or paprica, and beat it into the bubbling butter; let the mixture cook two or three minutes, then stir into it, rather gradually at first, and beating constantly, one cup of cold milk, water or stock. Now, when the sauce boils up once after all the liquid is in, it is ready for use. In making a white sauce some cooks add, from time to time while the sauce is being stirred, a few drops of lemon juice, which they claim makes the sauce much whiter.

Sometimes we make the sauce after another fashion, using the same proportions of the various ingredients. If water or stock be used, put it in the blazer directly over the fire. If the liquid be milk, put it into the blazer, and the blazer over hot water; cream together the butter, flour and seasonings, dilute with a little of the hot liquid, pour into the remainder of the hot liquid, and stir constantly until the sauce thickens, and then occasionally for ten or fifteen minutes, until the flour is thoroughly cooked.

In making a brown sauce, first brown the butter, then brown the flour in the butter, and, whenever it is convenient, use brown stock as the liquid.

### Ingredients for One Cup of Sauce.

- 2 tablespoonfuls of butter.
- 2 tablespoonfuls of flour.
- ¼ a teaspoonful of salt.
- A few grains of pepper.
- 1 cup of liquid.

### Ingredients for One Pint of Sauce.

- ¼ a cup of butter.
- ¼ a cup of flour.
- ½ a teaspoonful of salt.
- ¼ a teaspoonful of pepper.
- 1 pint of liquid.

## Measuring.

In all recipes where flour is used, unless otherwise stated, the flour is measured after sifting once. When flour is measured by cups, the cup is filled with a spoon, and a level cupful is meant. A tablespoonful or teaspoonful of any designated material is a level spoonful of such material.

## Flavoring.

When rich soup stock, flavored with vegetables and sweet herbs, is at hand for use in sauces, additional seasonings are not necessary; but when a sauce is made of milk, water, or water and meat extract, some flavor more or less pronounced is demanded. A few bits of onion and carrot browned in hot butter, or anchovy sauce or curry may be added; but, all things considered, the most convenient way to secure an appetizing flavor is by the use of "Kitchen Bouquet." This alone or in conjunction with a dash of some one of the many really good proprietary sauces on the market is well-nigh indispensable in chafing-dish cookery.